AF560681

DEVELOPMENT OF EDUCATION SYSTEM IN INDIA

Edited by
Dr. A R. Rather
Department of Education
Kashmir University
Srinagar

DISCOVERY PUBLISHING HOUSE
NEW DELHI-110002

Published by:

DISCOVERY PUBLISHING HOUSE PVT. LTD.
4383/4B, Ansari Road, Darya Ganj
New Delhi-110 002 (India)
Phone : +91-11-23279245; 23253475; 43596065
E-mail : discoverybooksindia@gmail.com
discoverypublishinghouse@gmail.com
web : www.discoverypublishinggroup.com

***First Published:* 2004**

***Reprinted:* 2021**

ISBN: 978-81-7141-816-9

Development of Education System in India

Printed at:
Infinity Imaging Systems
Delhi

Contents

Preface

Teachers' Training is a vital part of Education. Therefore, all efforts of the educationists, educators and instructors are aimed at the task of providing better training to the 'would be teachers' for their better education and proper growth, as a benefactor. No doubt, this responsibility can only be exercised, if the educators are equipped with the required knowledge of the subject concerned and the trainees develop needed interest in it. That's why, it becomes essential for making adequate provisions for each course to the teachers and as well as trainees. This series is designed for providing a solid practical base for all the papers. The series has been prepared strictly according to the B.Ed. syllabus, prescribed by universities.

Of course there are many a book on the subject, presently available in the market. But every author has his or her own style and way of presentation. The present work also has its own features, characteristics and significance. While preparing this series of books, the editor had to refer to the works of other authors and various sources for information. He expresses a deep gratitude for incorporating their ideas in the text. Hopefully, this series would serve as perfect reference material for all teachers, teacher-students and other readers also. If that much is achieved, the undersigned would feel contented and honoured.

–Editor

Syllabus

DEVELOPMENT OF EDUCATION SYSTEM IN INDIA

Unit I. Education in Ancient & Medieval India

(i) Vedic Education

(ii) Brahmanic Education

(iii) Buddhist Education

(iv) Muslim Education

Detailed description of salient features, objectives, curriculum, method of teaching, role of teachers related to these systems of education

Unit II. Education in British India

Detailed study of the following landmark documents :

(i) Macaulay's Minutes (1835)

(ii) Wood's Despatch (1835)

(iii) Indian Education Commission (1882)

(iv) Indian Universities Commission (1902) & Act, (1904)

(v) Gokhale's Bill (1910-12)

(vi) Sadler Commission Report (1917)

(vii) Govt. of India Act (1935)

(viii) Sargent Report (1944)

Unit III. Education in Post-independence Era

Detailed study of the following landmark documents :

(i) Radhakrishnan Commission (1948)

(ii) University Education Commission (1948-49)

(iii) Secondary Education Commission (1952-53)

(iv) Indian Education Commission (1964-66)

(v) National Policy on Education (1986)

(vi) Revised National Policy (1992)

Unit IV. Problems & Issues — I

(i) Universalization of Elementary Education

(ii) Women's Education

(iii) Distance Learning

(iv) National & Emotional Integration

Unit V. Problems & Issues—II

(i) Medium of Instruction

(ii) Education of Weaker Sections

(iii) Adult Education

(iv) Quality Control in Higher Education.

1

Vedic Age

In India, history of education began with the Vedic period. Vedic education is linked more with ancient period i.e. from 2000 BC to 200 BC. Ancient period is said to have come to a close with the fall of great king Harsha in 647 AD. Medieval period is considered as the closing period of Vedic education. Vedic studies during 747 AD to 1200 AD declined. The observations of Prof. Taneja point out that systematic system of education in India must have begun with Vedic period when Aryans had entered into Indian soil.

Salient Features

Aim of Education. Aim of education in India was to develop various aspects of life and also to ensure social service.

Rig Veda. According to Rig Veda, "Education is something which makes a man self-reliant and self-less.

Upanishads. According to Upanishads, "Education is that whose end product is salvation."

Vedantic View. According to Vedantic point of view, "The essence in man is spirituality. We need education that quickens, that verifies, that kindles the urge of spirituality inherent in every mind".

Religious Imitation. Education in the first epoch (period of time in history) of the ancient period (2000 BC — 200 BC) was nearly a religious imitation and teacher laid emphasis to teach the pupils bow to pray how to offer sacrifices and perform other duties according to the system of life.

Upnayan or Ceremony Related to Taking the Child to Guru. The children of the castes (brahmin, kshatriya or vaishya) used to initiate their education after performing a ceremony entitled as Upnayan i.e. taking child to the Guru for the purpose of education of the child. Guru used to give the Guru Mantra (Savitri Mantra) to the student & then start his education.

Age for Education. There are differences on the fixation of age for initiating education in the Ashram of a Guru. The age for Upnayan Ceremony may be 8, 11 or 12 yrs. in case of Kshatriyas, Vaishya and Brahmin. Shudras were not allowed for education.

Duration of Education. The general duration of education was twelve years. Only one type of veda can be studied during the span of 12 yrs. Students used to select one veda out of four for their education. Ten years duration was sufficient for studies in literature and religious education.

Duration of the Session. About four and half or five and half months in a year were developed for the purpose of studies (generally from Shrawan to Poomima).

Time of Education. No specific time has been mentioned for time table. Studies were generally undertaken in the morning, noon and evening after lunch break.

Educational Buildings. No specific information is available on the type of educational building. It is assumed that classes were used to be held under trees, but literature reveals that there were buildings or specific structures for Gurukuls.

Gurukul System of Eucation. Gurukul system of education is very prominent feature ofVedic education. Students used to live in the Ashram of Gurus for the purpose of education. Gurukuls were situated in natural surrounding and away from cities.

Student Life. (1) Food: Meal was provided only two times (morning & evening). There was no provision of food in-between because the uptake of food during mid day is not good for health and spiritual development. Vegetarian food was used to be served only. (2) Dress for Students: There were different dress codes for brahmin, kshatriya and vaisay students. Beaotification of the body was not allowed. (3) General Code of Conduct of Students.

* Student were supposed to be:

— disciplined and

— self-controlled

* They used to get up early in the morning.
* They were required to perform morning and evening prayers.
* "Havan" was an important activity.
* Students who used to opt for studies of Veda had to devote more time in Havans. Memorisation activities were more. Morning, noon evenings were devoted for academic activities.
* Respect for teachers.
* Restriction for telling lies and passing undesirable remarks for any one.
* Brahamacharya was very important for students.
* Students were not allowed to keep money with them.
* They were not allowed to buy any item.
* They were not allowed for music, dance and gambling *(Drul Krida).*
* They were not allowed to talk much with females.
* They were instructed to control sex, anger and greed.
* They were supposed to live a simple life. They were not allowed to talk about their caste, wealth, position etc. They used to live under common living conditions of the Ashram/Gurukul.

Duties of Students towards

* Students used to place Gurus at high level, even better than that of their parents and God. Guru was considered as spiritual father.
* They used to stand up in me honour of their Gurus & used to sit at the lower level.
* Service of the Guru was considered to be supreme.

Duties of the Guru towards Students. Gurus used to treat their students as their own family members.

* They used to impart education for all round development of the students.

They used to put in their best for inculcating in their students good habits, feelings of sacrifice, social service and development of skills useful in their later life.

Punishment. Generally, punishments were not given but under special conditions of student behaviour, minor corporal punishment or other sorts of punishments are mentioned in the literature.

Free Education. There was free education. There was a tradition of giving *"Dakshhia"* after completion of the education. Students used to offer Dakshina as per their family positions as a mark of respect for the teacher (Guru).

Autonomy of Gurukuls/Ashrams. There was no control of any ruler or a member of society on Gurukuls/ Ashrams. The Gurukuls were the residential areas of Gurus. They used to be spiritual scholars. Brahmins used to render free educational service to the masses.

Education in ancient India was free from any external control like that of the State or the Government or any party politics. It was one of the king's duties to see that learned pundits pursue their studies and their duty was to impart knowledge without interference from any source, what soever. So education did not suffer from any communal interest or prejudices in India.

Curriculum. A variety of subjects were used to be taught. For example:

* Study of all the four Vedas
* Study of Puranas & Upanishads
* History & examples from history
* Science of numbers
* Science of time
* Logic
* Moral science
* Etymology
* Ceremonial and religious practices
* Ayurveda (Indian system of medicine)

* Art of teaching for interested & intellectual students (This was for die purpose of developing skills to perform duties as Gurus in their later life).

Individualistic Pattern of Education. Method of Education was individualistic. Each guru had his own students.

Women Education. Full attention was given on women education during vedic period.

Vocational Education. Comparatively, there was less emphasis on vocational education as compared to spiritual and religions education during Vedic period. Education in the following vocations was imparted during vedic period:

* Purohit Education for Brahmins for performing religious social activities.
* Military education for Kshatriya
* Commerce & trade education for Vaishyas
* Seven year medical education. Ayurveda or Indian System of Medicine was very popular during 250 BC to 800 AD.
* Vocational training in various fields was also available.

Aims of Education

Spiritual Aim. Knowledge of Self and the God (Absolute) Self-realisation/self-knowledge and knowledge of the Absolute, the Almighty or God was the chief aim of education. Ultimate aim of this knowledge is the union with Almighty. So, knowledge was considered as an instrument of salvation. Some of the major concepts are listed as follows:

* Unity of moral and spiritual outlook
* World reality & self reality
* Law of karma
* Transmigration
* Sara. bondage, ignorance and the true knowledge
* Moksa or liberation and unity of sadhna
* Pranayama as medium of true knowledge.

Divinity of Nature. Nature was regarded as divine and was worshipped.

Control over Materialistic Outlook. There was emphasis on the control of materialistic tendencies.

Individual Character Building and Personality Development.

* Right conduct
* Self-control
* Self-respect Cooperation
* Sympathy

Social Aim.

* Development of socially acceptable behaviours
* Obedience
* Discipline

Vocational Aim. Enabling the individual to acquire practical skills for earning livelihood.

Preservation and Transmission of Cultural Values. The vedic values were preserved and transmitted through education as an instrument.

Performance of Ritual. Performance of rituals was considered essential.

Curriculum

Curriculum during vedic education was linked with me following aspects:

1. Vedic literature and grammar: Rigveda; Yajurveda; Samaveda & Atharva Veda
2. Puranas
3. Spiritual aspect: Soul, self. God; divinity of nature etc.
4. History & stories based upon important aspects of life and personalities
5. Arithmetic & Geometry
6. Astronomy

7. Philosophy
8. Logic
9. Ethics
10. Conduct
11. Rituals
12. Understand and implementation vedic aphorisms (principles or maxims)
13. Medicine (Ayurveda)
14. Military science
15. Agriculture
16. Animal husbandry
17. Arts & crafts
18. Construction
19. Sculpture
20. Commerce and Trade
21. Yoga
22. Administration
23. Diplomacy

Methods of Teaching

Following methods of teaching were used during vedic period of education:

1. Recitation method
2. Discussion method
3. Question-Answer Method (Reasoning can be developed using question-answer techniques)
4. Illustration with examples (drashtanta)
5. Memory methods (emphasized by Aitreya Brahman Gautam)

   (1) Steps for Memorisation & Correct Pronunciation
   * Memorisation of lesson

* Meditation on the contents
* Emphasis on pronunciation

(2) Factors that Affect Memory and Reasoning

Memory depends upon following factors (Nyayasutra of Gautam):

— Attention
— Recall
— Intuition (abhigyana)
— Association of ideas
— Recollection.

6. Pronunciation Methods
7. Meditation Methods
8. Apprenticeship (child used to learn parental profession and language at home.

Role of the Teacher

1. Teacher (the guru) was used to be a spiritual personality. There was a direct contact between the guru and students. Students used to contact gurus and receive education as per their perception of education.
2. Routine duties were generally performed by the students while living with the gurus.
3. Teacher used to teach & make general arrangement for students for required life style.
4. Teachers used to be encouraging in their attitudes.
5. Teachers used to be scholars in many areas e.g.
   * Philosophy
   * Methodology of acquiring knowledge
   * Grammar
   * Astrology
   * Many other subjects.
6. Teachers used to behave with students as their own children.

7. Teachers were used to develop me personality of their students in accordance with aims of education.
8. Teachers used to put emphasis on the development of the personality of the individual.
9. Teachers were used to develop in students a desire of education.
10. Students were taught to realise their responsibilities towards parents, society and the guru.
11. Teachers were used to teach social skills to the students.
12. Teachers were used to develop self-study habits in their students.
13. Teachers were used to examine or evaluate students orally.
14. Teachers were used to develop skills related to military science, agriculture, animals husbandary, medicine, arts and crafts, chemistry, commerce etc.
15. Teachers were used to imitate their gurus.
16. Teachers were used to develop vocational skills also. Teachings requirements were different depending upon the requirements of different sections of the society. Goals of education based upon different sections of society.

Section of the Society.	*Subject Offered / Goals*
1. The Kshatriyas	— Study of Logic — Study of Vedas — Training in Military Science — Princes were taught — Sankhya Yoga — Public Administration
2. The Vaishyas	— Diplomacy — Agriculture — Animal husbandry

— Trade

— Commerce

— Agriculture

3. The Shudras — Trade

— Animal husbandry

— Cow care

— Manufacture of weapons

— Construction

— Sculpture

— Drawing & Painting

— Others

QUESTIONS

1. Describe various salient features of vedic education.
2. Discuss briefly various aims of Vedic education.
3. Write on the curriculum during Vedic education.
4. Discuss the methods of teaching in the system of Vedic education.
5. Describe the role of the teacher in the system of Vedic education.

2

Brahmanic Age

After Vedic education, Brahmanic education is a refined and developed form of vedic education only. The period of brahmanic education is considered to begin in 200 BC. During this period, intellectual activities in various fields of literature and worldly or material subjects were undertaken. Some important personalities of this period are Kalidas (the author of Shakuatalam), Arya Bhatta (originator of Algebra) and Hand (a great patron of teaming and education who contributed a lot for the development of primary education). Primary schools were connected with temples. Village communities supported schools.

Salient Features

Emergence of Various Form of Educational Limitation. Various forms of educational institutions were developed during this period e.g.

1. Shakha
2. Charana
3. Parishad
4. Kul
5. Gotra
6. Ashramsin forest

Creation of Classical Texts. Classical texts were written by scholars during this period.

Sutra Literature and Six Indian Philosophies.

(1) Sutra literature was created during this period

(2) Six systems of philosophies also developed during this period:

* Samkhya
* Yoga
* Nyaya
* Vaisheishika
* KaramorPurva Mimansa
* Vedanta or Uttara Mimansa

Education as a Weans of Knowledge but Dominance of Religious. Education like vedic education was instrument of acquisition and understanding the spiritual, physical, social and religious education dominated in the Brahmanic education system.

Curriculum: Significant changes occured in this direction as syllabus was determined according to caste and Asharam system.

(1) **Vedas.** The study of vedas was given first priority. People developed blind faith in vedas.

(2) **Other Subjects**

* Sanskrit
* Grammar
* Arithmetic
* Geometry
* Astrology
* Economics
* History
* Politics
* Agriculture
* Military Science
* Nyaya philosophy

(3) Emphasis was given on the study of philosophy.

Methods of Education.

* Oral methods of teaching
* Memory-Methods (students were required their explanations).
* Written Methods also developed during Brahmanic period as writing developed. Bhojpatra is the baric of a tree. Practice in writing was given to students.
* Pronunciation Methods

* Discussion Method
* Question-Answer Method
* Practical Method.
* Listening, Contemplation, Comprehension, Self-study & recall methods.

Physical Punishment. Physical punishment was not favoured by acharyas like Manu, Gautam, & Vishnu.

Brahmcharya (Celibacy). Emphasis was given to Brahm Charya (Celibacy).

Aims of Education

* Physical development of the individual
* Mental development of the individual.
* Character development

Free and Universal Education. There was free and universal education.

* No role of administration on political parties in the control of education.

Decline in Women Education & Education of Shutrax. A decline was observed in the education of women & shudras during Brahmanic period.

Varna System. Varna system got transformed into rigid caste system.

Sanskrit was the language of conversation.

Aims of Education

1. Development of physical, social, intellectual and spiritual aspects of the personality of an individual.
2. Intellectual freedom.
3. Development of understanding of religious, spiritual and material aspects.
4. Transmission and preservation of Indian values.
5. Self-control

6. Development of character
7. Development of social awareness.

Curriculum. Studies were mainly focussed on the following subjects :

1. Sanskrit
2. Indian scriptures like vedas, puranas & other classical texts.
3. Indian philosophies
4. Material world
5. Religious studies and rituals
6. Literature
7. Astrology
8. Medicine (ayurveda)

Methods of Teaching. Schools were linked with temples. Brahmins were considered knowledgeable and used to impart education using traditional recitation methods & some practical ways of life to teach varied aspects of life.

Role of the Teacher

Free Education. Teachers used to offer free education.

Teaching was based on Community Needs. Teachers were the guides of the society and used to impart instruction on those lines which were important during those days i.e. spiritual development, social relations, intellectual development etc.

Increase in Ritualism. Rituals were important for the society and teachers used to guide the society in these aspects also. There was gradual increase in ritualism

Psychology of the Learner. Teachers used to impart education depending upon the requirements of the students. Nature, interests and tendencies of learners were kept in view by teachers.

Punishment. Corporal punishment was not given by learners but this was rarely used.

QUESTIONS

1. Describe salient features a Brahmanic education.
2. Discuss brahmanic education under the following headings:
   (a) Aims of education
   (b) Curriculum
   (c) Methods of teaching
   (d) Role of the teacher.
3. Comment upon the following:
   (a) Celibacy and Brahmanic education
   (b) Aims of education of Brahmanic educaton.
4. Discuss the aims of education and the role of the teacher with specific reference to Brahmnic education.
5. Describe curriculum and methods of teaching in context of Brahmnic education.
6. Give a comparative account of vedic education and Brahmanic education.

3

Buddhist Age

As compared to Brahmanic education, Buddhist education system was not rigid in rituals. People got attracted towards this system. The common man women, castes like preferred this system. The educational centres of higher learning developed. The present chapter deals briefly a few aspects of Buddhist education.

Salient Features

Founder of Education System. Buddhist education system (200 B C to 200 A D) was founded by Lord Gautama Buddha of the Sakayas.

Four Noble Truths. Buddha mentioned the following four noble truths:

(1) The noble truth is that there is suffering or misery.

(2) The second noble truth is that there is a cause of misery.

(3) The third noble truth is that there is cessation of misery.

(4) The fourth noble truth is that there is a path leading to the cessation of misery.

Teachings. Teaching of Buddha are:

(a) All things are conditional. There is nothing that exits by itself.

(b) All things are, therefore, subject to change owing to the change of the conditions on which they depend. Nothing is permanent.

(c) There is, therefore, neither any soul nor God or any other permanent substance.

(d) There is, however, continuty of the present life which generates another life by the law of Karma just as a tree generates another tree through the seed, and the second continues while the first withers away.

Buddhist Education. A Reaction to Vedic Ritualism during Brahmanic Period — People were not happy with the excessive emphasis on rituals during the Brahmanic Period. Brahmanic Education deprived common man and especially, women and shudras from education. Buddhist Education offered to impart education to all. People shifted to Buddhist system of education.

Age of the Student.

(a) Generally one could begin education at the age of eight.

(b) The student used to remain in a state of 'sharamana' till the age of 12.

(c) At 20, the student was used to be qualified to become monk.

Medium of Instruction. Pali was the medium of instruction. Local languages of various regions were also encouraged.

Pababja Ritual for Initiating Eduction. A ritual called as "Pababja ritual" was necessary for admission to a monastry for education. Educational period far this phase was twelve years. Student was used to called as 'shramana'.

Features of the ritual are listed briefly below:

1. One had to get his head shaved, wear yellow clothes and place one's head at die feet of die monks living in die monastry and sit cross-legged. One was then required to repeat die following sentences thrice :

   (a) I take refuge to Buddha
   (b) I take refuge to Itecma
   (c) I take refiige to Sangha.

2. Lastly, one was required to obey following certain rules:

   Abstain from:

   (a) Theft
   (b) Killing of any living being
   (c) Impure conduct

(d) Partaking of food at prohibited times
(e) Use of intoxicating things
(f) Use of cosmetics
(g) Taking things without being offered
(h) Accepting objects of gold and silver in alms.
(i) Watching dancing or listening of music

Upsamapada Ritual. After 20 Years of Age. Upsampada ritual is performed at the age of twenty. The education after this ritual was of ten years duration. Presence often moirics was me time at ceremony. Male monks were now called as "Bikshu" and female ones as "Bikshuni." Certain rules were to be followed by Bhikshu and Bhikshunis e. g.

(1) To live under a free

(2) To eat only the food available to the begging bowls.

(3) To drink urine of the cow as medicine.

Duties of a Student

(1) Service to teachers & to develop parental relations with teachers.

(2) To beg for alms

(3) To eat food thrice a day

(4) To wear three items of cloth

(5) To take bath in pure water

(6) To maintain discipline

Women Education. Women were allowed to join sanghas/ monasteries. Separate women monasteries were also opened. Women were also sent to other countries to spread Buddhism. One of the famous name was Sanghmitra who was sent to Ceylon.

Vocational Education. Vocational education was imparted in certain areas e.g. writing, agriculture, commerce, animal husbandry, archery, magic, etc.

Primary and Higher Education. Education was organised at the primary and secondary levels. Age of admission at primary level was six years "intermediate education was the main focus at this stage. Higher level of education was also provided in the monasteries and universities. Students used to come from other countries e.g. Korea, Tibet, Java etc.

Development of Specific Centres of Education-Centres of Buddhist education developed. Feelings of democratic outlook developed. Viharas, monasteries and universities came into existence for imparting education. Universities developed at Taxilla, Nalanda, Balabhi, Vikramshila, Odant puri, Nadia and Jagdalla.

Contribution of Buddhist Education.

(1) General education of children got significant position in the society.

(2) Practical subjects got priorities in teaching & learning. Respect developed for manual & practical skills.

(3) The group teaching and provision of a number of teacher in an institution started from this period.

(4) Universities established during this period are still serving as a guiding forces e.g admission age, rules etc.

(5) Education as a social institution got its existence as a result of Buddhist system of education.

Comparison of Vedic Education and Buddhist Education

The account of Vedic education and Buddhist education is given in below.

TABLE

Difference Vedic Education and Buddhist Education

Vedic Education	*Buddhist Education*
1. Centres of Education	
Teacher's house or Gurukul was the centre of education.	Educational centres were viharas, monasteries and universities.
2. Medium of Education	
Sanskrit was the medium of education.	Praakrat was the medium of education.
3. Teacher &. Caste	
Brahmans were used to perform the role of leaders	Teachers were selected among the monks. There was no consi-

in the society.	deration of caste as in the case of vedic education.
4, Availability of Education to Society	
Education was the right of Brahmans, Kshatriyas, Vaishya only.	No consideration of any caste Education was available to every individual irrespective of caste, or any other factor.
5. Fee	
Education was free	Fee was there in one form or the other.
6. Aims of Education	
* Individual development * Social development * Spiritualism * Knowledge of vedas * Puranas, etc. * Vocational education.	* Personality development * Democratic living * Faith in the teaching of Buddha. * Nirvana as the aim of education
7. Curriculum	
Study was centred around over vedas, puranas, upanishad, rituals, personal & social development.	Study was equally centred material studies & religions leading to Nirvana. Practical/ manual skill development subjects were given importance.
8. Methods of Teaching	
Recitation method, discussion method, question answer method, memory method were important.	Recitation method, discussion method, practical methods & question and answer methods were common.

Aims of Education

1. Knowledge aim

   (a) Teaching of Buddha

   (b) Material aspects of life

   (c) Practical skills

2. Development of Personality
3. Social development Aim. (upliftment of downtrodden)
4. Vocational development aim.
5. Religious aim
6. Character development aim
7. Nirvana i.e the final liberation is the highest end of human existence.

Curriculum

Primary Education/General Education/Religious Education. Age for admission to primary education- or general education was six year. Following aspects were important for general education of children :

* Religious concept
* Concepts on material world
* Learning about Siddhirastu which contained 49 words
* Writing
* Medicine
* Social service
* General behaviour or conduct. Pali as a medium of instruction.

Vocational Education Curriculum. The demand for technical and science education was not less than that of general education or religious education.

1. Knitting & Sewing
2. Building Construction
3. Sculpture
4. Drawing and Painting
5. Accountancy
6. Agriculture
7. Commerce

8. Cottage Industries
9. Animal Husbandry
10. Elephant Love
11. Magic Charms
12. Astrology

Higher Education. Higher education centres imparting Buddhist education included education in the following areas:

1. Buddhism
2. Hinduism
3. Jainism
4. Philisophy
5. Metaphysics
6. Logic
7. Sanskrit
8. Pali
9. Astrology
10. Astronomy
11. Medicine
12. Law
13. Polity
14. Administration

Taxilla University. Taxilla was the capital of Gandhara and was an important centre of higher education. Taxilla was named after the name Taxa, the son of the king Bharata. Taxilla university/ provided education in the following subjects:

1. Three vedas
2. Vedanta
3. Grammar
4. Ayurveda
5. Military Science

6. Astrology
7. Agriculture
8. Commerce
9. Treatment of Snake bite
10. Magical Charms (TantraVidya)

Nalanda University. The Nalanda University was situated in Bihar. Most of the subjects offered at Taxilla university were a part of the curriculum. Some areas of specialisation are listed below:

1. Mahayan, a school of Buddhism
2. Hinayana
3. Vedic life, Jain religion
4. Vedas
5. Vedanta philosophy
6. Purana
7. Medicine

Ballabhi University. A famous centre of Buddhism (475 AD to 775 AD in Kathiavar). This centre was famous for the study of following subjects:

1. Politics
2. Diplomacy
3. Medicine
4. Various other Studies apart from religious studies.

Vikramshila University. Vikramshila was situated on the banks of Ganga, in Magadha, Bihar. This centre was famous for academic activities for translation of religious text into Tibetan language.

Main subjects offered in studies were as follows: -

1. Grammar
2. Logic
3. Philosophy
4. TantraVidya

Mithila and Nadia Universities.

1. Nyaya
2. Philosophy
3. Logic

Methods of Teaching

There was no teaching by Guru as in the case of Vedic education but teacher were selected from the monks and teachers used various institutional methods e.g.

1. Discussion Method
2. Question answer Method
3. Oral Methods
4. Memorisation Methods (emphasis was on memorisation)
5. Debate to quote Guwar Myrdai. "Scholastic debates were encouraged. Such learned assemblies were a new feature of Buddhist higher education."
6. Logic
7. Analytic Methods
8. Narrations & Clarifications
9. Simple explanation of the text
10. Practical methods for acquiring practical skills.

Role of the Teacher

1. There were good relationships between teachers and students. To quote A.S. Altekar

   "The relations between the novice and his teacher were filial in character; they were united together by mutual reverence. Confidence and affection."

2. A variety of methods were used by the teacher to impart religious as well as material & professional education.
3. Various languages were used as media of instruction because this helped students who used to come from various parts of the country.

4. Teacher's personal life was simple and a model for the students.
5. Teachers themselves were scholars and they continuously chanced their teaching competencies and knowledge.
6. Teachers used to do their best to develop various facilities for the students.
7. They used to lead a disciplined life.

QUESTIONS

1. Describe salient features of Buddhist education.
2. Comment upon the following in context of Buddhist education:

   (1) Pababja ritual

   (2) Upsampada ritual

   (3) Higher education
3. Give a comparative account of Vedic education and Buddhist education.
4. Discuss aims of education and the role of the teacher with specific reference to Buddhist education.
5. Describe curriculum at various levels of Buddhist education.
6. Comment upon the curriculum at the following universities:

   (1) Taxilla University

   (2) Nalanda University

   (3) Ballahi University
7. Discuss Buddhist education with specific reference to aims of education, curriculum, methods of teaching and role of the teacher.

4

Muslim Period

During Muslims period, educational development (about 700 years) was slow because before Akbar development in education was mostly dependent upon the interests of the ruler. Akber & Jahangir took comparatively more interest in the development of Muslim education. Education during Muslim period was founded on community basis. Rulers mostly propagated education on the basis of their interests and ambitions. Muslim education could not touch the heart of public life because of political and social factors. Government protection was also not sufficient. The present chapter describes salient features, aims, curriculum, methods of teaching and role of the teacher in Muslim Education.

Salient Features

Community based Education. Madarsa and maktabs were associated with mosques. Rulers helped these educational set ups depending upon their interests. Some rulers granted Jagirs or landed property. Scholars were given honzourable place in the courts of rulers.

Teaching of Arabic and Persian & Emergence of Urdu.

(1) Special emphasis was given on the teaching of Arabic and Persian language.

(2) Arabic and Persian languages were the media of education,

(3) Arabic and Persian were essential for official employment.

(4) Urdu developed as a new language as a result of inter-mixing of Arabic and Persian. Emergence of Urdu is the significant contribution of Muslim period.

Writing of Muslim and Mughal History. Rulers attached importance to writing of history of their times. Some important write-ups/manuscripts are: Babar Nama, Akbar Nama etc.

Islam Based Education. Education was influenced by Islam. Educational objectives were to search the Islamic knowledge. Students were required to memorise Holy Koran.

Education for Earning Livelihood. Practical skills in various areas (sculpture, house construction, weapon construction, etc.) were taught by experts individually. Learners learnt these skills in varied areas as apprentices. Overall purpose of learning the practical skills was to earn the livelihood.

Teachings were Based on Koran. Islam had its origin between 570 A.D. and 632 A.D. Hazrat Mohammad collected his messages in the Holy Koran and this text was used by rulers for social change.

Contribution of Muslim Rulers.

(1) Mohammad Gauri and his successor Kutubudin constructed mosques and schools in Ajmer for teaching Islam and Muslim law. Rulers of Slave dynasty like Iltutmish, Razia Begum, Nasiruddin and Balban also helped in opening maktabs and schools.

(2) Tughlak dysnasty also paid attention towards opening of schools, Ferozshah Tughlak opened a school in Delhi. Governmental aid and scholarships were given.

(3) Sikandar Lodi (1489-1519) attached importance to the involvement of Hindus in administration. Indian languages were given importance. Urdu developed during this period.

(4) Mughal rulers (Akbar & others) paid more attention to education. Translation of Indian scriptures like Mahabharat, Ramayan, Athaervaveda, Lilawati etc. was done in Persian language. Emphasis was given on the following:

* Moral values
* Arithmetics
* Agriculture
* Medicine

* Logic
* Physical Methematics
* Divine Philosophy

(5) Jahangir enacted a law that property and wealth of any person , who had not legal heirs, would be utilized for the repair of schools and religious buildings.

(6) Shahjahan established a University near Jama Masjid.

(7) Aurangzeb destroyed Hindu schools & temples and provided facilities for Muslim students.

Educational Centres. Important centres of Muslim education were : Agra, Delhi, Jaunpur, Lahore, Ajmer, Bidar, Ferozabad, Jullundar, Multan, Bijapur.

Agra. It was founded by Sikandar Lodi. This city was established as a centre of Muslim education. Madrasras provided education in literature, Mathematics, Philosophy, Medicine etc. Akbar, Jahangir and Shahjahan also contributed to the development of education at this place.

Delhi. Nasiruddin established Nasaria madrasa here. Gulam dynasty took interest in the development of Muslim Education. There were 34 muslim scholars in Delhi during the rule ofAllauddin Khilji. Thirty madrassas were opened by Feroz Tughlak. Humayun opened madrassas for astrology and geography. Madarsas for specific fields were also opened by Akbar, Jahangir, Shahjahan and Aurangzeb.

Jaunpur. Jaunpur was the important Centre of muslim education during the rule of Feroz. Education in arts, literature and other fields was imparted. Shershah Suri was a student of the center at Jaunpur.

Bidar. Mahmood Gawan and Allauddin developed Bidar as a center of Muslim education. Mahmood developed a library at Bidar.

There are a number of other places and regions e.g. Bijapur, Golkunda, Malwa, Khandesh, Multan, Gujarat, Lucknow, Sialkot and Bengal, where at least one **Maktab** and one **Madarsa** was opened in each village.

Organisation. Organisation of Muslim education is shown here.

Muslim Education (Levels)

Bismillah	*Maktab*	*Madrasas*
* Education began with the ritual (performed at home) known as *Bismillah* * Age : 4 yrs. * Maulvi (the teacher) recites recitation from Koran arithmetic, drafting, conversation & letter-writing etc. were taught.	* It is a primary school * Teaching of alphabets & verses by the *Maulvi* (the teacher) * Maktabs were attached with mosques * Koran, prayer (Namaz), azaan, by private bodies as well as by Govt.	* Centres of higher learning * Aided by Government * Lecture method was used * Hostel arrangements were made * These educational centres were there.

Organisational Structure of Muslim Education

Bismillah. (A Ritual at the Age of 4). It was the ritual which was used to be performed by a Maulvi (teacher) when the child attained the age of 4 years, 4 months and 4 days. Maulvi used to recite me relevant recitation from Koran.

Maktab (Primary School). Maulvis (teachers) used to teach alphabets and verses from Koran. These were generally attached with mosques. "Main areas of education were : Koran, namaz (prayer), azaan, arithmetic, drafting, conversation and letter-writing.

Madarsa. There were the centres of higher learning. These were aided by Government. Lecture method was followed. Hostel arrangements were there for students. Private as well as Government bodies were the owners of there centres.

Merits

Merits of Muslim education (which continued about 500 years) can be listed in the following lines:

Development of Vocationalisation. Vocationalization or professionalisation developed as a result of synthesis of materialism and religious education.

Employment Opportunities for Educated Individuals. State services were given only to educated persons.

Emphasis on Utility Based Education. Education was not for the sake of knowledge only but for the practical utility. Aurangzeb was in favour of education of princes.

Education was Compulsory for Muslim. Hazrat Mohammad (Pbuh) was of the opinion that receiving education was akin to achieving God. He who attains education attains God.

Emphasis on History & Writing of History. Roots of history writing can be considered from Muslim period. Emphasis was given on the writing of history and teaching of history.

Teacher student Relationship. Good Relationship were there between teachers and students.

Demerits

1. Emphasis on Material aspects of education, Religious aspects were comparatively less covered.
2. Only rich/affluent section of the society recieved education.
3. Woman education was neglected.
4. Emphasis was only on reading and writing.

Aims of Education

Objectives of Muslim education changed with changes in the interests of Muslim and Mughal rulers. Objectives of education, however, can be listed broadly as follows :

Strengthening of Political Position and Administration. Education was being imparted to strengthen the political position of rulers and to employ educated employees for smooth running of the administration. According to Jafar, a few evidences in this context are listed here:

The posts of Wazirs (Ministers) and Kazis (preachers) were reserved for educated persons. As a result of this attitude of rulers, many Hindus got the Muslim education and rose to high positions.

Preparation of the Individual for Future Life. Preparation of an individual for the future life was also one of the aims of muslim education.

Religious Knowledge for Salvation. One of main aim of Muslim education was to spread the religious knowledge to masses for the purpose of achieving salvation.

Propagation of Religious Knowledge. Rulers wanted to spread muslim religious knowledge.

Propagation of Muslim Law & Muslim Value System. Masses were informed about Muslim laws and shariyats of the holy Koran through Muslim education. This aim of Muslim education helped rulers to srengthen their positions in context of social and political ends or objectives of administration.

Curriculum

Major areas of Muslim Education are listed below (Bhatnagar 1983):

1. Koran
2. The biography of Hazrat Mohammad (Pbuh)
3. History of the laws of Islam
4. Arabic and Persian languages
5. Grammar
6. Literature
7. Logic
8. Philosophy
9. Law
10. Astrology
11. History
12. Geography
13. Agriculture
14. Unani system of medicine.
15. Sanskrit for Hindu children

Methods of Teaching

General Methods of teaching were as follows :

1. Memory Methods for memorisation of various aspects of knowledge.
2. Recitation Methods
3. Reading Methods
4. Writiisg Methods
5. Oral Methods
6. Monitor Methods in maktabs and madarsas.'

Role of the Teacher

1. Teachers were used to be holy persons and teachers of the society at large.
2. Teachers used to develop the personality of the students using different methods.
3. They used to follow the principles of reward and punishment.
4. Medium of instruction used by teachers was Arabic and Persian. After the growth of Urdu education was used to be imparted through it.
5. Student-teacher relationships were harmonious. Teachers used to behave like parents.

QUESTIONS

1. Discuss various salient features of Muslim education.
2. Comment upon the following :

   (1) Contribution of Muslim rulers.

   (2) Educational centres
3. Discuss the organisation of Muslim education.
4. Describe merits and demerits of Muslim education.
5. Discuss Muslim education with specific reference to aims of education, curriculum, methods of teaching and the role of the teacher.

6. Give a comparative account of Buddhist Education and Muslim Education.
7. Discuss higher education both in Buddhist education and Muslim education.
8. Discuss the types of educational centres is Vedic, Brahmanic, Buddhist and Muslim education.
9. Discuss teacher in context of Vedic, Brahmanic, Buddhistic and Muslim education.
10. "Curriculum and Muslim Education." Comment briefly.

5

British Period

(1835-1947)

Macaulay's Minute (1835)

The views of Macaulay are known as Macaulay's Minute (1835). The Minute was submitted on 2nd of February, 1835. Maculay came to India as on the 10th of June, 1834 as Law Member of Governor General's (Lord William Bentick) Council. Views of Macaulay sought by Lord William Bentick on the following clause included by British Parliament in the Charter of The East India Company:

"To the effect that after defraying all civil and military expenses, a sum of not less than one lakh of rupees in each year shall be set apart and applied to the revival and improvement of literature and the encouragement of learned natives of India and for the introduction and promotion of knowledge of science among the inhabitants of the British territories in India."

Main Points Covered in the Macaulay's Minute

1. British system of education was considered better as compared to ancient Indian education system.

2. The meaning of the word "literature" mentioned in the Charter of the company (1813) was taken as English literature. It was considered that Sanskrit, Arabic or Persian have no literature of their own.

3. The meaning of "learned natives of India" was taken in the sense that the natives of India who have read the philosophy of Locke and who are familiar with the poetry of Milton.

4. Indian literature was criticised heavily as is evident from the following writing of Macaulay:

   "A single shelf of a good European library was worth the whole native literature of India and Arabia."

5. English was recommended as the medium of instruction and Indian languages were rejected as a medium of instruction on the account that they are under developed and lack scientific vocabulary. English was declared the best among the languages of the West. English helps on the access to intellectual wealth of the world. He writes the following:

   "It stands prominent even among the languages of the West. Whoever knows that language, has ready access to all the vast intellectually wealth which all the wisest nations of the earth have created."

6. Aim of education should be to develop such personalities who are Indians in blood and colour but English in taste, in opinions, in morals and intellect.

To quote Macaulay.

"We want a class of persons, Indians in blood and colour, but English in taste, in opinions, in morals and in intellect."

Bentick's Proclamation on Macaulay was issued in 1835

Proclamation is stated below :

"The great object of the British Government would henceforth be the promotion of European Literature and Science through the medium of English and that all Government funds appropriated for the purpose of education would be best employed on English education alone."

Wood's Despatch (1854)

Sir Charles Wood was the President of the Board of Control to Government of India. He submitted a report on the reformulation of education policy in India in 1854. This report is popularly known as Wood's Despatch.

Recommendations

1. Creation of Department of Public Instruction in each province.

2. Director of Public Instruction will be the head of Department of Public Instruction.
3. Universities should be established to hold examinations and award of degrees.
4. Open the teachers training colleges.
5. Open the high schools.
6. Useful and practical knowledge suited to every situation of life should be imparted in educational institutions.

Actions Taken on the Recommendation

1. Department of education was created in each state/ province.
2. Director of Public Instruction was appointed as Head of the Department of Education.
3. Three Universities each in Calcutta, Madras and Bombay were opened in 1857.
4. High Schools were opened under the control of these universities.

Indian Education Commission (1882)

Hunter Commission

Indian Education Commission (1882) is also known as Hunter Commission. The education in India was reviewed & recommendations were submitted.

Recommendations

1. Secondary education, as far as possible, be provided on the grants-in-aid basis and that the Government should withdraw, as early as possible, from direct management of secondary schools.
2. The Government should take the entire responsibility of primary education leaving secondary education to private enterprise.
3. Diversified courses of instruction should be introduced. There should be two avenues, one leading to the entrance

examination of the University and other of a more practical character intended to fit the youths for commercial, vocational or non-literary short measure pursuits.

Indian Universities Commission (1882)

Act (1904)

Indian Universities Commission was appointed by Lord Curzon for the purpose of educational standard in five Indian Universities—Calcutta, Madras, Bombay, Allahabad and Punjab.

1. Improvement in the quality of Instruction in Indian Universities.
2. Schools were recognised by the universities uader Indian Universities Act (1904).

Gokhale's Bill (1910-12)

Indian leaders began to point out the need of education in India since 1880. Indian National Congress which was established in 1885 also gave strength to the views of Indian leaders for education in India. Gopal Krishna Gokhale was the member of the Imperial Legislative Council and as a member he moved the resolutions in the Council on March 19,1910. The Council recommended that a beginning should be made in the direction of making elementary education free and compulsory throughout the country.

Council introduced the first draft of law for compulsoty education for age-group 6-10. He pleaded that universal, free and compulsory education was essential for the development of the country and Government should provide adequate funds for this purpose. Gokhale withdrew the resolution on the basis of assurance from the Government to consider the matter seriously. Department of education was organized under the Central Government but no steps were taken to make primary education free and compulsory. Gokhale introduced a Bill on 16th March, 1911 to provide for gradual introduction of the principle of compulsion into the elementary education system of the country. Efforts of Gokhale failed but he could focus the attention of the public on education and on compulsory education in particular.

Gokhale Resolution

1. Compulsory education should be introduced in the area of those local bodies where a certain percentage of children are attending schools.
2. Local bodies should obtain the consent of the Government before introducing compulsion.
3. Local bodies will have right to introduce compulsion in whole or the specific areas.
4. Local bodies can levy the cess to meet the cost of education.
5. Guardians of boys between 6-10 should be required to send their wards to recognized primary schools. In case of non-compliance they should be punished.
6. In due course of time, primary education should be made compulsory for girls also.
7. Those guardians whose monthly income is less than Rs. 10 should not be asked to pay fees.

Though the bill was not passed in the council but the developments in the council in this context could help in focussing the public attention on the need of compulsory elementary education in India. As a result of this, resolution was passed in 1913 in which some important points were: standards of institutions, provision of practical curricula for primary and middle schools and provision of better facilities for research in Universities.

Sadler Commission (1917)

Sir Michael Sadler was the Vice-Chancellor of Leads University. He was appointed Chairman of the Calcutta University Commission on 14th September 1917. The Sadler Commission is also known as Calcutta University Commission (1917-1919).

Secondary Education : Recommendations

1. Secondary education should be improved as this is the base for university education.
2. Admission to University should be on the basis of intermediate rather than matriculation.
3. Intermediate colleges should be started. Degree courses should be of three years.

4. Tutorials and seminars should be organised.
5. Variety of courses should be there—medical, engineering, agriculture, commerce, science and arts.
6. Medium of instruction should be any Indian language (mother tongue) up to High school stage. English should be the medium of instruction in Mathematics and English.
7. There should be a Board of Secondary and Intermediate Examination. Universities should be relieved of the work for secondary and intermediate education. The Board was required to:

    * frame curricula
    * hold two examinations at secondary level
    * recogne intermediate colleges.

8. Better emoluments for teachers
9. Improved system of examination
10. Student discipline
11. Better extra curricular activities.

Higher Education : Recommendations

1. Control over universities should not be rigid.
2. Selection Committee for selection of University teacher should include experts from outside also.
3. There should be bodies like Court and Executive Council instead of Senate and Syndicate.
4. Academic Council should be there to deal with matters on curriculum.
5. There should be three years degree course after Intermediate. Pass courses and Honours Courses should be there.
6. There should be a provision of diversified courses : Engineering, medical, law, agriculture, technical courses, etc.
7. Encouragement for education of Muslims keeping in view their backwardness in education.

8. Appointment of Director of Physical Training for organising activities with the aim to take care of health of the students.

Recommendations: Specific to Calcutta University

1. Establishment of Unitary Teaching University at Dhaka. In the light of increased enrolment at Calcutta University, a unitary teaching University at Dhaka may be opened. This was recommended to reduce the number of students at Calcutta University.
2. Increase in University Centres.

   The number of colleges outside Calcutta city should be increased.
3. The Calcutta University may be developed into an affiliating university.
4. The teaching resources should be re-organised.

Women Education

1. Opening of Purdah Schools.

   Purdah schools should be opened in the light of the need for education of girls between the age group 15-16.
2. Establishment of special Board of Women Education in Calcutta University.

   A special Board of Women Education should be established keeping in view the needs of women. The courses specific to women requirements should be started. Teachers training courses, medical courses etc. should be opened.

Teacher's Training Colleges

1. Education as a subject at the intermediate and graduation level (i.e. B.A.)
2. Opening of Education Departments at Calcutta and Dhaka Universities.
3. Increase in the number of trained teachers

Technological Education

1. Teaching of Applied Science and Technology at the University level.
2. Degrees and Diplomas in applied Science and Technology should be awarded on the completion of the designed courses.

Professional and Vocational Education

1. Professional and Vocational Courses should be opened.
2. Courses at the Intermediate Level should be revised to provide a scope for professional and vocational courses.

Establishment of Inter-University Board.

Establishment of Inter-University Board was recommended to develop a required co-ordination among various Indian Universities.

The above recommendations were implemented and as a result this educational scenario of India both at the university & school levels changed towards positive side. Women education, professional education, technical education, vocational education, teacher training colleges, school education, diversification of courses, science and technology education etc. got the due attention. Calcutta University and other Indian University could discharge two major functions—firstly that of centres of research and higher learning and second as affiliating universities.

Sargent Report (1944)

Sir John Sargent was the educational adviser to the Government of India. Central Advisory Board of Education assigned Sir John Sargent the task of reviewing post war educational developments in India and asked to submit the report popularly kown as "Sargent Report (1944).

Recommendations

1. Provision of universal, compulsory and free education for children of the age group 6—1 4.

2. Provision of a variety of courses for five years after the age of eleven. High schools should be of two types : academic and technical.

QUESTIONS

1. Describe the salient features ofMaculay's Minute (1935).
2. Comment upon the following :

   (1) Maculay's Minute (1935)

   (2) Wood's Despatch (1954)
3. Comment upon the following :

   (1) Hunter Commission (1882)

   (2) Indian Universities Commission (1902) and Act (1904)

   (3) Gokhale Bill (1910-12)
4. Describe in detail the recommendations of Sadler Commission (1917).
5. Discuss Sadler Commission (1917) with specific reference to higher education in mdia.
6. Discuss the following with specific reference to secondary education in India:

   (1) Wood's Despatch (1954)

   (2) Indian Education Commission (1882)

   (3) Sadler Commission (1917)

   (4) Sargent Report (1944)
7. Discuss the following regarding primary education in India:

   (1) Indian Education Commission (1882)

   (2) Gokhale's Bill (1910-12)

   (3) Sargent Report (1944)
8. Discuss the recommendations of the following for the development of higher education in India:

   (1) Wood's Despatch (1854)

   (2) Indian Education Commission (1882)

(3) Indian Universities Commission (1902) and Act 1904

(4) Sadler Commission (1917)

9. Describe the educational developments in India from 1935-1947 with specific reference to improvement at the primary and secondary levels.

10. Discuss important developments in the field of higher education from 1854 to 1917.

6
Modern Era

Following independence, Education in India was given due attention. The needs of the country were taken into consideration. The steps were taken in this direction. First major step was the setting up of University Education Commission (1948-49) under the Chairmanship of Dr S. Radhakrishnan. Secondary education was considered as the weakest link in the total educational scenario in India. As a result of this observation, Secondary Education Commission (1952-53) was set up for the improvement of secondary education. Significant recommendations were given by this commission. The present chapter highlights the main recommendations with specific reference to Universtity Education Commission (1948-49) and Secondary Education Commission (1952-53).

University Education Commission (1948-49) (Radhakrishnan Commission)

After independence in 1947, the University Education Commission was appointed in 1948, with Dr. S. Radhakrishnan, our late President, as its Chairman for the purpose of improving University education in India. It is also known as Radhakrishnan Commission.

Recommendations

Admission : University. Intermediate or equivalent qualification should be minimum qualification for admission to Universities.

Reforms at the Secondary Education Level. Secondary

education was viewed at that time the weakest link in the educational machinery and to improve university standards, the improvements at secondary level is a must.

To Quote Commission: "Secondary education is the weakest link in our entire educational machinery and needs urgent reform."

Examination Reforms. To quote Commission on examination reforms:

"If we are asked to give one single reform in university education, we shall say, it should be that of examination."

The reforms are required on various aspects of examination e.g. appointment criteria of examiners, experts, paper setters, marking (scoring) i.e. evaluation system; organisation, conducting of examination, etc.

Curricular Reforms. Following points should be taken into consideration for curricular reforms at higher level:

(1) Environmental problems of the learner

(2) Effective use of the language (medium of instruction)

(3) Application of basic principles of science

(4) Appreciation for values of life

Reforms in Research and Teaching

1. Teaching standards must be improved. Following suggestions were given :
    * Use of current methods of teaching
    * Ban on private candidates
    * Evening colleges should be opened
    * Provision for refresher courses for teachers
    * Standard text books
    * Good library facilities
    * Workshops should be organised for students
    * Good laboratories
    * Increase in teaching hours
    * Admission procedures should be improved
2. Research facilities should be strengthened so that universities may perform their role as research centres besides teaching centres.

Professional Courses. Better facilities should be provided for professional courses in various areas e.g. agriculture, engineering, technology, law, medicine etc. Opening of vocational and professional bodies was encouraged.

Facilities for Teaching Staff. Following points were emphasized in context of facilities for teaching staff:

(1) Improve salaries of the teaching staff

(2) Terms and conditions of service should be improved e.g. there should be a provision for provident fund, house facilities, fixation of working hours. vocations, etc

Secondary Education Commission (1952-53)

Government of India appointed Secondary Education Commission on September 23, 1955 on the advise of Central Advisory Board of Education. Dr. Lakshaman Swami Mudaliar, the then Vice-Chancellor of Madras University, was appointed the Chairman of the Secondary Education Commission. The commission is also called as Mudaliar Commission. The Commission was appointed to achieve the following aims :

1. To study the present position of secondary education in India.
2. To suggest measures for the improvement of secondary education taking into consideration following aspects:
   * Aims
   * Curriculum
   * Administration
   * Relationship of secondary education with elementary /basic education and higher education.
   * Interrelationship of various types of schools.
   * Problems of secondary education in India.

Problems

No Commission appointed before independence studied problems of secondary education as a whole. The Indian Education Commission 1882, Commission of 1902, the Sadler Commission of 1917 and even Radhakrishnan Commission (1948)'dealt only a few aspects of secondary education. Secondary Education mentioned the following defects in Indian education system :

1. The education given in our schools is isolated from life.
2. It is narrow, one sided and fails to train the whole personality of students. Non-cognitive aspects of personality (aptitudes, emotions, appreciation, etc.) are largely ignored.
3. English being the medium of instruction and compulsory subject of study, students do not possess special linguistic ability and are handicapped in studies.
4. Methods of teaching being used do not develop independence in through or initiative in action.
5. Increase in class size has reduced the contact between the teacher and the student.
6. Examination system is defective. It discourages all types of experimentation on the part of teacher.

Aims

Education for Development of Democratic Citizenship

1. Development of capacity for clear thinking and receptivity to new ideas. Development of scientific attitude of mind to enable one to think objectively and base one's conclusions on data.
2. Clearness in speech and writing. This will help in discussion, persuation and peaceful exchange of ideas.
3. All round development of personality taking into consideration psychological, social, emotional and practical needs.
4. Qualities should be cultivated for the purpose of discipline, social sensitiveness and tolerance.
5. Development of a sense of true patriotism. True patriotism involves three things—appreciation for social and cultural achievements of the country, a readiness to recognize its weaknesses frankly and to worl for their eradication and an earnest resolve to serve it with *Sue* best of one's ability, harmonizing and sub ordinating individual interests to broader national interests.

Education for Improvement of Vocational Efficiency of Learners

1. Greater emphasis on crafts and productive work. .
2. Diversification courses should be introduced so that a large number of students could benefit from it.

Girls schools and Co-education schools should be opened for solving the problems of women education. Special provision for study of Home Science should be there.

Languages

1. Mother tongue or the regional language should generally be the medium of instruction throughout the secondaiy school stage subject to the provision that for linguistic minorities special facilities should be made available on the lines suggested by the Central Advisory Board of Education.
2. During the middle school stage, every child should be taught at least two languages. English and Hindi should be introduced at the end of the Junior Basic Stage subject to the principle that no two languages should be introduced in the same year.
3. At the High and Higher secondaiy stage, at least two languages should be studied. One of which being the mother tongue or the regional language.

Curriculum

1. The present curriculum is narrowly concieved.
2. It is bookish and theoretical.
3. It is over crowded, without providing rich and significant contents.
4. which should reasonably find room in it if it is to educate the whote of the personality.
5. It does not cater to the various needs and capacities of the adolescents.
6. It is dominated too much by examinations.

7. It does not include technical and vocational subjects which are necessary for training the students to take part in the industrial and economic development of the countiy.

Recommendations

1. At the Middle, stage, the curriculum should include:

   Languages; Social Studies ; General Science; Mathematics; Art and Music; Craft; and Physical Education.

2. At the High School or Higher Secondary Stage, diversified courses should be provided for die pupils.

3. A certain number of core subjects should be common to all students whatever the diversified courses of study that they may take. These should consist of Languages, General Science, Social Studies, Maths, aad Craft.

4. Diversified courses of study should include the following seven groups: Humanities ; Sciences.Technical subject; Commercial subjects;

   Agricultural subjects ; Fine Arts ; Home Science. Additional diversified courses may be added depending upon the need.

5. The diversified curriculum should begin the second year of the High School or Higher Secondary School Stage.

Textbooks

A High-Power Textbook Committee should be constituted.

A part of the amount out of the sale of the books should be used for awarding scholarships, and providing books. and other amenities for school children.

Frequent changes in textbooks should be encouraged.

Methods of Teaching

1. Methods of teaching in school should not only aim at imparting of knowledge in an efficient manner, but at inculcating desirable values and proper attitudes and habit of work in the students.

2. Methods should be able to develop attachment to work and as desire to do it efficiently and thoroughly.

3. Activity methods and project methods should be used as these will reduce vetbatism and memorisation to learning. Useful, concrete and realistic situations should be provided.
4. Emphasis should be on clear thinking and clear expression in speech and writing.
5. Such method should be used that demand the acquisdon of knowledge through initiative and personal effort.
6. Group activities/group projects should be used to develop qualities necessary for group life and co-operative work.
7. There should be a provision of well-equipped school library, class library and subject library. In order to popularise progressive teaching methods and facilitale then introduction, "Experimental" and "Demonstration" schools should be established.

Character Building

1. **Discipline**
   (1) Education of character should be responsibility of teacher and school programs should be organized for this purpose.
   (2) Personal contact between teachers and students should be strengthened. This will promote discipline. House system, monitors and student council, code of conduct etc. should be integral part of the school .
   (3) Group games and other extra curricular activities should be organized.
2. **Religious and Moral Education.** Religious instruction may be given in schools only on a voluntary basis outside the regular school hours. Such instruction should be confined to the children of a particular faith and permission of parents is a'must.
3. **Extra-curricular Activities**
   (1) Extra-curricular activities be the integral part of education
   (2) There should be organisation of scout camps in school. Financial assistance for this should be given by the State.

(3) Activities related to the NCC, first aid, Red Cross etc. should be encouraged.

Guidance

1. Attention towards educational and vocational guidance should be given.
2. Visits to industries should be organized to develop awareness about nature of different work.
3. Services of trained guidance officers and career masters should be provided gradually.
4. The Centre should make efforts to establish centers where training in guidance and counselling is given to teachers and other guidance personnel

Physical Welfare

1. Health Education

(1) School medical service should be built in all states.
(2) There should be a medical check up and treatment of students.
(3) Training to teachers in first aid.
(4) Proper nutritional standards should be maintained in hostels of residential schools.
(5) Proper sanitation of the area.

2. Physical Education

(1) Physical activities should be organized for developing physical endurance.
(2) All teachers below the age of 40 should participate in physical activities of students.
(3) Record of physical education activities should be maintained.

Evaluation

1. Number of external examinations should be reduced. There should be only one public examination at the completion of secondary course.
2. Subjectivity in essay type tests should be minimised and objective type tests should be introduced.

3. Record of every student should be maintained.
4. Credit should be given for record of the student and internal tests.
5. The system of symbolic rather than numerical marking should be adopted for evaluating and grading the work of the Pupil's external and internal examination and in maintaining the school records.
6. System of compartmental examination should be introduced at the final public examination.

Teaching Personnel

1. General Improvements

1. There should be uniform system for the selection and appointment of teachers for all types of schools.
2. There should be selection committee in the privately managed schools.
3. Probation period of a teacher should be one year.
4. Teachers in a high school should be graduate with a degree in education. Teachers of higher secondary classes should have higher qualifications as prescribed for teachers of intermediate colleges in some states.
5. Special committee should be appointed to review scales.
6. Triple benefit scheme , pension-cum-provident fund-cum-insurance should be introduced to relieve teachers from anxieties of old age.
7. Arbitration Boards or Committee should be set up to deal with grievances of teachers.
8. Age of physically fit teachers may be extended to sixty.
9. Free medical attention is required.
10. Leave rules should be uniform.
11. Practice of private tuitions should be abolished.
12. Emoluments for the post of headmaster should be attractive. This will attract good persons.

2. Teacher Training

1. There should be two types of institutions for teacher training:

   1. Two year training after Higher Secondary School leaving certificate.

   2. One year training after graduation It should be extended to two years.

2. Graduate teacher training institutions should be recognised and affiliated to universities for the grant of degrees. Secondary grade teacher training institutions should be under the control of a separate board.

3. Training colleges should organize refresher coursers, workshops, seminars etc.

4. Research activities should be carried out.

5. Stipends for students should be there.

6. No tuition fee should be charged in training colleges.

Administration

1. Committee/Boards

(1) Director of Education should advise the Minister.

(2) There should be a constitution of committee consisting of Minister and other members. This committee will discuss matters like available resources for education.

(3) Co-ordination committee should be there to suggest improvements and expansion of education.

(4) A sub-committee for examination should be there.

(5) The Central Advisory Board of Education should continue to coordinate education in states. Toe State Advisory Boards should be created.

2. Inspection of Schools

(1) The inspector should study problems and suggest improvements.

(2) Inspectors should have high qualifications.

(3) There should be a pannel of experts with the inspector.

3. Management and Conditions of Recognition of Schools

(1) There should be well defined standards for recognition of schools.

(2) There should be managing boards of schools.

(3) Management Board will decide the salary, leave conditions etc.

(4) Fees fixed by schools should be approved by Department of Education.

(5) Number of students in each class should be limited.

4. School Building and Equipment

(1) Secondary schools should be established in rural areas with sufficient population.

(2) Transport facility should be available to students in urban areas.

(3) Ten square feet area is to be provided to each student in the classroom.

(4) Optimum number of students in a class should be thirty. It should not exceed forty. The total strength of the school should be 500 or maximum 750.

(5) These should be constructed in line with provision of diversification of courses.

(6) Expert committee should be appointed for suggestion on equipment.

5. Hours of Working and Vacations.

(1) Schools should decide school hours according to local conditions.

(2) Working days should not be less than 200 days. Working hours per week should be 35 periods of 45 minutes each.

(3) Regular 6 days working should be there.

(4) Summer vacation of 2 months. Two breaks of 10 to 15 days & other holidays.

Finance

1. Industrial education cess should be levied which should be used for technical and vocational education at the secondary stage.
2. A certain percentage of the net revenue from nationalised industries or concerns such as Railways, Communications, Posts and Telegraph, should be made available for the promotion of technical education.
3. Contributions for the development of secondary education should be exempted from the operation of the Income Tax Act.
4. Surplus funds from the religious and charitable endowments should be diverted to educational purpose.
5. All educational institutions should be exempted from the levy of property taxes.
6. Purchasing of equipments, books, etc. should be exempted from custom duty.
7. Centre should give financial aid for the reorganisation of secondary education.

QUESTIONS

1. Describe the recommendations of University Education Commission (Radhakrishnan Commission), for the improvement of higher education in India.
2. Describe any three major problems of secondaiy education in India and recommendations made by Secondary Education Commission (1952-53).
3. Discuss problems of secondary education as mentioned by secondary Education Commission. Describe the following problems and the recommendations made by S.E.C., (1952-53).

   (a) Aims of secondary education

   (b) Curriculum

   (c) Methods of teaching

4. Comment upon the following:

   (a) Language problem and recommendation of SEC

   (b) Recommendation of SEC regarding character building.

5. Comment upon the following with specific reference to Secondary Education Commission (1952-53).

   (a) Improvement of teaching personnel.

   (b) Organisation and administration.

6. Discuss the following in the light of Secondary Education Commission:

   (a) Health and Physical Education of the learners

   (b) Evaluation of the learner

   (c) Educational and vocational guidance of the learner.

7. Discuss briefly the aims curriculum, methods of teaching and teacher education in the light of Secondary Education Commission (19.2-53).

7

Education Commission

After indenence, the Indian Education Commission (1964-66) was the third one in continuation of Radhakrishnan Commission (1948-49) and Secondary Education Commission (1952-53). So, during twenty years of independence adequate attention was paid to education at all levels (primary, secondary and higher education). Before independence, the first Indian Education Commission or Hunter Commission was set up in 1882. Second one was in 1902 & the third one was in 1917 (Calcutta University Commission). The comparison of the three commissions before independance and after independance highlight the educational developments during 65 yrs. (1882-1947) the developments during seventeen years (1947-1964). The present chapter deals with problems of Indian education and recommendations for improvements in line with Indian society in general.

Setting up of the Commission

Indian Education Commission was set up on 14th July, 1964. Professor D.S. Kothari, the then Chairman of University Grants Commission, was appointed as Chairman of the Indian Education Commission. The Commission is also known as Kothari Commission.

The inauguration of the Commission was held on 2nd October, 1964 in the Vigyan Bhavan. The then President of India, Dr. S. Radhakrishnan in his message said.

"It is my earnest desire that the commission will survey all aspects of education-primary, secondary, university and technical and make recommendations which will lead to improve our educational system at all its levels.

Rationale

1. Indian values should be preserved and transmitted effectively.
2. Needs of modern Indian society should be taken into consideration.
3. There was a difference in the thought and action in the area of education.
4. Development of democratic values was required.
5. There was a need for development of secularism.
6. Technological development was needed.
7. There were many problems at all the levels. The problem of universalisation of primary education was the challenging one. Vocationalisation of secondary education was another. Similarly at the higher level quality was the significant question.

Problems

1. Expansion of scondary schools
2. Curriculum
3. Teaching methods
4. Textbooks, teacher's guides and teaching materials
5. Class size
6. School buildings
7. Guidance and counselling
8. Search for and development of talent
9. Backward children
10. Evaluation and examinations
11. School organisation and administration
12. Supervision
13. State institute of education
14. State and national boards of education

15. The educational structure
16. Finance.

Recommendations

Expansion of Schools. Problems of expansion at the secondary stage are

1. Problem of establishment of secondary schools.
2. Problem of enrolment in secondary schools.
3. Problem of planning and location of schools.

Recommendation in the light of above problems of expansion of secondary education are described here.

Problem of Establishment of Secondary Schools

(1) Consolidation if secondary schools.

(2) Creation of the school of a size that is economic and efficient.

(3) Slow down the proliferation of small and uneconomic schools.

(4) Establishment of new schools should be only in areas where a clear local need can be proved.

(5) Establish a secondary school serving a radius of five to seven miles within the total population coverage of 10,000 to 15,0000.

(6) Institutions of vocational education should be large in size, economical and efficient.

(7) Careful plans are required for the location of educational institutions.

(8) Separate schools should be established for girls.

Problems of Enrolment in Secondary Schools

(1) Broad Principles of Enrolment

(1) Overall enrolment in secondary schools should be broadly governed by the need for trained man-power.

(2) Enrolment for vocationalisation of secondary education is essential. About 20 per cent of the

enrolment should be at the lower secondary and about 50 per cent of that at the higher secondary stage.

(3) There should be emphasis on equalisation of opportunities in secondary education. Enrolment of girls, S C & S T should be encouraged.

(2) Enrolment for Part Time Education: Facilities for part time education should be provided in general and vocational courses. Enrolment targets should be 20 per cent of the total enrolment at the lower secondary stage and 25 per cent at the higher secondary stage.

(3) Enrolment of Girls: Efforts should be made to accelerate the expansion of girl's education so that the proportion of girls to boys reaches 1 : 2 at the lower secondary and 1:3 at the higher secondary stage in 20 years.

Problem of Planning and Location of School

(a) A national policy for location of new institutions should be adopted.

(b) Establishment of small and uneconomic institutions should be avoided.

(c) Vocational schools should be located near the industry concerned.

Curriculum

1. Unified Approach

1. There is an explosion of knowledge. Reforms in curriculum are needed. A unified approach should be followed.

2. **Essentials of Curricular Improvement**

   (1) School curriculum should be developed through research findings.

   (2) There should be periodic revision and these should be research based.

   (3) Textbooks and teaching-learning materials should be developed.

   (4) In-service teacher education programs should be organised for orienting the teachers.

(5) Schools should be given freedom to devise and experiment.new curricula.

(6) Ordinary and advanced curricula should be prepared by State Board of School Education.

Organisation of the Curriculum

1. Common curriculum of general education should be provided for the first ten years in non-vocational schools. Specialisation and diversification should begin at the Higher Secondary level.
2. Courses will be diversified at the Higher Secondary stage. A student will study a group of any three subjects in depth. Half of the time will be provided to electives, one-fourth to the languages, one-fourth to Physical Education, Arts and Crafts, and Moral and Spiritual Education.
3. Enrichment program for talented students should be there.
4. Provision of ordinary and advanced courses should begin with class VIII. In the beginning advanced courses in Mathematics, Science and Languages should start at the Lower Secondary Stage and in all subjects at the Higher Secondary stage.

Study of Languages

1. Lower Secondary Stage (VIII-X) is the suitable stage for learning three languages. The modified three languages should include:
   (a) The mother tongue or the regional language.
   (b) The official language of the Union or the associate official language of the Union so long as it exists.
   (c) The Modern Indian or European language not covered under (1) and (2) above and other than that used as the medium of instruction.
2. At the Higher Secondary Stage, two languages will be compulsory.
3. A nation wide program should be organized for the promotion of Hindi on a voluntary basis.

4. Study of classical languages such as Sanskrit or Arabic should be encouraged.

Science and Mathematics Education

1. Science and Mathematics should be taught on a compulsory basis to all pupils as a part of general education during the first ten years of schooling.

2. At the lower secondary stage, Science should be developed as a discipline of mind. Current concepts of Physics, Chemistry and Biology should be included and experimental approach to learning these concepts should be followed.

3. Talented students should be provided advanced courses in selected schools.

4. Science teaching should be linked to Agriculture in rural areas and to Technology in urban areas.

5. In Mathematics, current concepts should be included. Logical thinking should be emphasized.

6. Modern methods of teaching Science and Mathematics should be used, *e.g.* investigatory approach. Guide material for teachers should be there. Flexibility in the curriculum should be there to cater to the needs of students.

Social Studies

1 Social studies teaching is important for the development of good citizenship and emotional integration.

2. Syllabus should stress on national unity and the unity of man.

3. The scientific spirit and method of the social sciences should permeate the teaching of Social Studies at all stages.

Work-experience

1. Work-experience should be in the form of workshop training at the lower secondary stage.

2. Work-experience at the Higher Secondary Stage should be provided in the school workshop, farm or commercial and industrial establishment.

3. Teacher training, preparation of instruction material, mobilisation of local resources should be taken up

Social Service

1. Programs of Social Service and participation in community development should be organised.
2. Labour and Social Service camps should be organised.

Physical Education

Physical Education programs should be reformed on the principles of child growth and development. Physical Education is important for the physical fitness and efficiency, mental alertness and development of certain qualities of character.

Education in Moral and Spiritual Values

Moral education should be imparted. Spiritual values should be inculcated through ethical teachings of great religions. One or two periods per week should be devoted.

Creative Activities

A variety of co-curricular activities should be organised to provide opportunities to students for creative self-expression.

Curricula for Boys and Girls

There should be no differentiation of curricula for boys and girls. Commission endorses the Mehta Committee recommendations. Home Science should be optional paper but not compulsory. Provision should be there for Music and Art. Study of Science and Mathematics should be encouraged.

Teaching Methods

Teaching methods should be modernised and new methods based upon research should be used to meet the intellectual requirement of a variety of school going children. We have failed to modernize our teaching methods due to following reasons :

1. The competence of an average teacher is poor.
2. There is no proper research on teaching methods in the light of our needs.

3. Our educational system is rigid. It does not encourage initiative, creativity and experimentation.
4. There is a problem of diffusion of dynamic methods of teaching in our educational system.
5. It is recommended that elasticity and dynamism in the educational system can only help us in providing place to modern methods of teaching. *e.g.* problem solving methods.

Text Books, Teacher's Guides and Teaching Materials

1. A program of provision of quality textbooks and other teaching learning materials at a low cost should be there.
2. A comprehensive program of textbook production at the national level should be implemented. This will also be useful in national integration.
3. The preparation, and evaluation of textbooks should be the responsibility of the State Education Departments.
4. There should be continuous revision and improvement of the text-books.
5. State production of textbooks should be on no profit no loss basis.
6. Teacher's guide and other instructional materials should be supplied alongwith textbooks.
7. List of minimum teaching aids and equipment should be provided to schools.

Class Size

1. The number of students in lower secondary classes should be restricted to 45.
2. The number of students in higher secondary classes should be restricted to 40.
3. Research should be undertaken for multiple-class teaching.

School Buildings

(a) Allocations for construction of school buildings should be increased.

(b) Community resources should be mobilised on the basis of equalisation.

(c) Loans and grant-in-aid should be given on a liberal basis.

(d) Norms for spacing and planning of school building should be followed.

(e) Local initiative should be encouraged in rural areas.

(f) Nucleus approach should be followed in building construction.

Guidance and Counselling

1. Guidance and counselling should be regarded as an integral part of education. This will assist students to make decisions and adjustments.
2. Guidance at the secondary level school, among other things, helps in the identification and development of the abilities and interests of adolescent pupils.
3. A trained counsellor should be incharge of the guidance program.
4. A short range programme should be adopted for the next 20 years consisting of minimum guidance programme for a group of schools, comprehensive guidance programme in selected schools, one in each district, to serve as models.
5. Teachers should be given training in guidance.
6. Supervisory staff should be provided in State Bureau of Guidance.

Search and Development of Talent

1. Search for talent must be a continuous process.
2. A variety of extra-mural programs should be organized for the talented.
3. Teachers should be trained to deal with talented students.

Backward Children

1. The backward children should be identified and remedial programs should be organized for them.

2. Under achievers should be given due attention.
3. Parent Teacher Association and guidance programs should be used for the benefit of backward children.

Evaluation

Evaluation is a continuous process. It forms an integral part of the total system of education. Evaluation influences pupil's study habits and teacher's method of teaching. Two major recommendations are mentioned here.

1. Internal assessment by schools should be comprehensive and all aspects of the students should be evaluated.
2. Experimental schools should be set up where the school is authorised to follow its own curricula and evaluation methods. State Board of Education may issue certificate on the recommendation of the school.

School Administration

Qualitative improvement is possible through the solution of problems of school administration.

Sympathetic and Imaginative System : A sympathetic and imaginative system of administration is essential for initiative and accelerating educational reforms.

The Common School System of Public Instruction : A common school system of public education (excluding independent schools and unrecognised schools) should be followed over the next 20 years.

(a) Govt. and Local Authority Schools : A school committee with local representation should look after the management of every government and local authority schools or a group of schools in an area. Teachers should not be transferred too often. Greater freedom should be given to these schools.

(b) Private Schools : Private schools should be aided adequately: Each private school should have a management committee consisting of representatives of the management, the Education Department and teachers. Grant-in-aid should be improved. Staff should be appointed on the pattern of government or local authority schools.

(c) Good Quality Private Schools : Good quality private schools which abolish tuition fees under the common system should be given grant-in-aid.

(d) Scholarships : Scholarships at the school stage may be given by the Government and local authorities.

(e) Tuition Fee : Tuition fee be abolished in phased manner.

3. A Nation-wide Programme for School Improvement

(a) Each institution should be helped to grow its own individual pace.

(b) Motivation of human agencies should be emphasized more as compared to that of increasing physical resources.

(c) Schools will be classified on a three point scale.

(d) Admission will be made on merit basis.

Re-organisation of the State Department

The State Education Department will deal with educational matters. It will be responsible for development and implementation of a programme of school improvement.

Prescription and enforcement of standard; inspection and supervision; Establishment of State Institute of Education.

Supervision

1. Administration should be separated from supervision. District School Board will deal with administration. District Educational Officer will deal with supervision. There should be coordination between the two.
2. There should be two types of inspections : annual and triennial or quinquennial inspection. Annual inspection will be done by State Education Department, Triennial or quinquennial inspection will be done by State Board of School Education.

State Institute of Education

An academic wing will have to be developed in State Institute of Education to look after the in-service training of departmental officers, improvement of teacher education, curricula and text-books, guidance and evaluation and research.

State and National Board of Education

1. In order to secure continuous improvement in standards, an adequate machinery should be set up at the state and national levels.

2. Standards should be defined and prescribed by State Government. The State Evaluation Organisation and State Boards of School Organisation will assist in defining, measuring and periodically receiving these standards. 3. National Board of School Education will be established at the Centre to advise the Govt of India on all matters relating to school education.

The Education Structure

It will be advantageous to have a broadly uniform educational structure in all parts of the country. The ultimate objective should be to adopt the 10+2+3 pattern. The higher secondary stage of two years should be located in schools, colleges or both according to local conditions.

Finance

The aim should be gradually to increase the investment in education so as to reach a level of expenditure of 6 per cent of the national income as early as possible.

QUESTIONS

1. List various problems of education as pointed out by Indian Education Commission (1964-66).

2. Describe the recommendations of the Indian Education Commission (1964-66) on any two of the given problems:

   (a) Curriculum

   (b) Teaching methods

   (c) Administration

3. What is the difference between the recommendations of Secondary Education Commission (1952-53) and Indian

Education Commission (1964-66) with specific reference to Curriculum at the secondary level.

4. Comment upon the recommendations of Indian Education Commission on the problem of expansion of school education.

5. Comment upon the following:

   (a) Examination and evaluation.

   (b) Guidance and counselling.

8

National Education Policy

NPE or National Policy on Education (1986) was announced by Rajiv Gandhi on January 5, 1985. Certain factors were taken into consideration. For example, problems like national and social integration, preservation and transmission of Indian values, composite culture of Indian society, communication technology etc. were the basis of national policy. The policy could provide guidelines to all those who are linked with Indian education. The present chapter describes briefly salient features of the policy, and all the major aspects covered in the policy.

Rajiv Gandhi's Concept of National Development and NPE-1986

National Policy on Education-1986 (NPE-1986) was announced by Rajiv Gandhi on January 5, 1985 in his broadcast to the nation for the purpose of national development.

Rajiv Gandhi had in his mind some important factors of national progress in context of National Policy on Education-1986. His concept of national development in the context of NPE-1986 can be analysed on the basis of following developmental factors:

(1) Promotion of national cohesion.

(2) Development of work ethics.

(3) Freedom struggle and its significance for national integration.

(4) Ancient Indian heritage and culture.

(5) Curbing parochial and communal interpretation of our composite culture.

(6) Utilisation of new communication technology.

(7) Delinking of degrees from jobs under Government.

(8) Open education within the easy reach of all.

(9) Schools to act as centres of excellence.

(10) Education has relation with productive forces of society e.g., industry, agriculture, communication and other productive sectors of our economy.

To quote Rajiv Gandhi: "Education must promote national cohesion and the work ethics. The grandeur of our freedom struggle and its significance for national integration has to be brought home to every student. Our schools and colleges should acquaint the younger generation with India's ancient heritage and culture. The curricula and text-book should curb parochial and communal interpretation of our composite culture."

Salient Features

The document on The National Policy on Education has 12 parts and 157 paragraphs. Each part highlights specific feature of NPE-1986. Salient features of NPE-1986 are listed below :

The role of education has been specified under heads e.g. :

(a) "Education for all" is important for national development.

(b) Acculturation is essential.

(c) Manpower development is needed.

(d) Education as unique investment.

National system of education should be as follows :

(a) There should be a common school system.

(b) There should be a common educational structure i.e., 10+2+3

(c) National system of education should be based on the national curricular framework.

(d) Education system should develop international outlook.

Education for Equality

(a) There should be education for women's equality.

(b) Due emphasis should be there for education of scheduled castes.

(c) Greater attention is needed for minorities (educationally deprived or backward groups).

(d) Education must prepare handicapped to face challenges of life.

(e) Adult and continuing education (15-35) has been emphasized.

Reorganisation of Education at Different Stages. Reorganisation of education has been suggested on the following lines:

(a) National policy regarding early childhood care and education.

(b) National policy regarding elementary education.

(c) School facilities.

(d) Non-formal education.

(e) Secondary education.

(f) National policy on vocationalisation of education.

(g) Higher education.

(h) Open university and distance learning.

(i) Rural university.

(j) Delinking degrees from Government jobs.

Technical and Management Education

(a) Institutional thraut.

(b) Innovation, research and development.

(c) Promoting efficiency and effectiveness at all levels.

(d) Management functions and change.

Making the System Work

Reorienting the Content and Process of Education

(a) Cultural perspective.

(b) Value education.

(c) Languages.

(d) Books and libraries.

(e) Media and educational technology.

(f) Work experience.

(g) Education and environment.

(h) Mathematics teaching.

(i) Science education.

The Essence and Role of Education

Education for All: In our national perception, education is essentially for all. This is fundamental to our all-round development material and spiritual.

Acculturation: Education has an accularating role. It refines sensitivities and perceptions that contribute to national cohesion, a scientific temper and independence of mind and spirit—thus furthering the goals of socialism, secularism and democracy enshrined in our Constitution.

Manpower Development : Education develops manpower for different levels of the economy. It is also the substrate on which research and development flourish, being the ultimate guarantee of national self-reliance.

A Unique Investment : Education is a unique investment in the present and the future. This cardinal principle is the key to the National Policy on education.

National System of Education

The Constitution embodies the principles on which the National System of Education is conceived of. The concept of a National System of Education implies that up to a given level, all students, irrespective of caste, creed, location or sex have access to education of a comparable quality. To achieve this the Government will initiate appropriately funded programmes. Effective measures will be taken in the direction of the common school system recommended in the 1968 policy.

The National System of Education envisages a common educational structure. The 10+2+3 structure has now been accepted in all parts of the country. The national System of Education will be based on a national curricular framework which contains a common core alongwith other components that are flexible. All educational programmes will be carried on in strict conformity with secular values.

India has always worked for peace and understanding between nations, treating the whole world as one family. Education has to strengthen this world view and motivate the younger generation for international cooperation and peaceful co-existence. This aspect cannot be neglected. The nation as a whole will assume the responsibility of providing resource support for implementing programme of educational transformation, reducing disparities, universalisation of elementary education, adult literacy, scientific and technological research etc.

Education for Equality

The new education policy proposes to lay special emphasis on the removal of disparities and to equalise educational opportunity by attending to the specific needs of those who have been deprived of equality so far.

With a view to attain the above goal, the following aspects of education have been specially considered :

Education for Women's Equality: It has been laid down to use education as an agent of basic change in the status of women. The National System of Education will foster the development of new values through redesigned curricula, textbooks, the training and orientation of teachers etc. Women's studies will be promoted as a part of various courses and educational institutions encouraged to take up active programmes of further women development.

In addition to above, the removal of women's illiteracy and their retention in elementary education will receive over-riding priority. Major emphasis will be laid on women's participation in vocational, technical and professional education at different levels.

The Education of Scheduled Castes: The central focus in the scheduled caste educational development is their equalisation with the non-scheduled caste population at all stages and levels of education. Under the new policy, the following measures have been contemplated :

(a) Incentives to families to send their children to school regularly till they reach the age of 14.

(b) Pre-matric scholarship scheme for children of families engaged in occupations, and to cover through time-bound programmes.

(c) Special steps to provide non-formal education for the drop-outs.

(d) Constant micro-planning and verification to ensure enrolment, retention and successful completion of courses together with provision of remedial courses to improve their prospects for further education and employment.

(e) The recruitment of teachers from scheduled castes.

(f) Location of school-buildings, balwadis, and adult education centres in such a way as to facilitate full participation of the scheduled castes.

(g) The utilisation of the funds and resources so as to make substantial educational facilities available to the scheduled castes.

(h) Constant innovation in finding new methods to increase the participation of the Scheduled Castes in the educational process.

Minorities: Greater attention will be paid to the education of the educationally deprived or backward groups. This is necessary to maintain equality and justice. This will naturally include the constitutional guarantees given to them to establish and administer their own educational institutions, and protection to their languages and culture.

The Handicapped: The new policy proposes to integrate the physically and mentally handicapped with the general community as equal partners. It also expects them to face life with courage and confidence by preparing them for normal growth.

The following measures will be taken:

(a) Education of children with major handicaps and other mild handicaps to be common with that of others.

(b) Provision of special schools with hostels at district headquarters, as far as possible.

(c) Vocational training of the disabled.

(d) Reorientation of teacher-training programme to deal with the special difficulties of the handicapped children.

(e) Voluntary efforts for the children of the disabled.

Adult Education. The new policy has suggested a vast programme of adult and continuing education particularly in the age-group 15-35 through various ways and channels:

(a) Establishment of centres in rural areas for continuing education.

(b) Workers' education through the employers.

(c) Post-secondary educational institutions.

(d) Wider promotion of books, libraries and reading-rooms.

(e) Radio, television and films, as mass and group learning media.

(f) Creation of learners' groups and organisations.

(g) Programmes of distance education.

(h) Organising assistance in self-learning.

(i) Need and interest-based vocational training programme.

Early Childhood Care and Education

The National Policy on Education recognised the holistic nature of child development, viz, nutrition, health and social, mental, physical, moral and emotional development. Early Childhood Care and Education (ECCE) will, therefore, receive high priority and be suitably integrated with the Integrated Child Development Services (ICDS) programme, wherever possible. Day-care centres will be provided as a support service for universalisation of primary education to enable girls engaged in taking care of sibling to attend school and as a support service for working women belonging to poorer sections.

1. Child-oriented Programmes of ECCE will be child-oriented, focussed around play and the individuality of the child.

2. Integration of Child Care and Pre-primary Education: A full integration of child care and pre-primary education will be brought about, both as a feeder and a strengthening factor for primary education and for human resource development in general. In continuation of this stage, the school health programme will be strengthened.

3. Proposed Programme: ECCE will be in the first instance, directed towards the most privileged groups i.e. those who are still outside the mainstreams of formal education. Some of these can be defined as follows:

   (a) Very poor urban 'slum' communities.
   (b) Ecologically deprived areas where children are required to fetch fuel, fodder, water, and do other household chores much in the day time.
   (c) Family labour and household work in rural areas and artisan household.
   (d) Working children in the unorganised sector.
   (e) Seasonal labour who has a mobile and transient life style, like road-workers.
   (f) Construction workers in urban and rural areas.
   (g) Landless agriculture labour.
   (h) Nomadic communities and pastoralists.
   (i) Forest dwellers and tribals in remote areas.
   (j) Residents of remote and isolated areas.
   (k) Girls in these groups may require support services like child-care sometimes in very small units. Special attention should be given to scheduled castes and scheduled tribes in all the above defined categories.

Elementary Education

The new thrust in elementary education emphasizes two aspects:

(1) Universal enrolment and universal retention of children up to 14 years of age, and

(2) A substantial improvement in the quality of education. Child-central Approach. The policy framers believe that a warm welcoming and encouraging approach, is the best motivation for the child to attend school and learn. A child-centered and activity-based process of learning

should be adopted at the primary stage. As the child grows, the component of cognitive learning will be inceased and skills organised through practice. The policy of non-detention at the primary stage will be retained, making evolution as disaggregated as feasible. Corporal punishment will be firmly excluded. School timing as well as vocation will be adjusted to the convenience of children.

School Facilities. The new policy lays down that provision will be made for essential facilities in primary schools, including at least two reasonably large rooms that are usable in all weathers, and the necessary toys, blackboard, maps, charts and other learning material. At least two teachers, one of whom woman, should work in every school. They should increase as early as possible to one teacher per class. A phased drive symbolically called OPERATION BLACK BOARD will be undertaken with immediate effect to improve primary schools all over the country. Government, local bodies, voluntary agencies and individuals will be fully involved. Construction of school buildings will be the first priority in the provided funds.

Non-Formal Education (NFE)

Launching Systematic Programme of NFE: A large and systematic programme of non-formal education will be launched for school dropouts, for children from habitations without schools, working children and girls who cannot attend whole-day schools.

Utilizing Modern Techniques and Aids: Modern technological aids will be used to improve the learning environment to NFE centres. Talented and dedicated young men and women from the local community will be chosen to serve as instructors. Particular attention will be paid to their training. Steps will be taken to facilitate their entry into the formal system in deserving cases. All necessary measures will be taken to ensure that the quality of non-formal education is comparable with formal education.

Curriculum should be Related to the Needs of the Learners: Effective steps will be provided to develop a framework for the curriculum on the lines of the national core curriculum, but based on the needs of the learners and related to the local environment. Learning material of high quality will be developed and provided free of charge to all pupils.

Involving Voluntary Agencies: Much of work of running NFE centres will be done through voluntary agencies and Panchayati Raj institutions. The provision of funds for these agencies will be adequate and timely. The government will take overall responsibility for this vital sector.

Programme of Action

Implementation Strategies at the Elementary Level

Area Specific and Population Specific Planning: The central features of the implementation strategy will be area specific and population specific planning : About 75% of the out of school children are in nine States . Andhra-Pradesh, Assam, Bihar, Jammu & Kashmir, Madhya Pradesh, Orissa, Rajasthan, Uttar Pradesh and West Bengal. While these States have been treated as educationally backward, enough attention has not been paid in the past to educationally backward pockets and groups in other States. Sustained effort will be made to see that all backward areas and population pockets make progress.

Access to the Elementary Education: Children of all families in the country will be provided access to elementary education of good quality.

Removal of Disparities: In view of the role of education in removal of disparities, special measures will be taken to ensure that whatever the socio-economic background of the children they get opportunity to achieve success of a level which approximates to the level of children from comparatively better-off sections of society.

Nation-wide Programme of School Improvement: A nation-wide programme of school improvement, with required multi-level and multidimensional planning, will be launched to alter the present situation of institutional stagnation and social apathy.

Centrality of the Child: The country's faith and its future generations will be exemplified in the system of elementary education, which will get geared around the centrality of the child.

Whole-time Schools: For the healthy development of schools and to ensure that they enjoy conditions of freedom and dignity, the education system will strive to have all children in whole time schools of good quality, and till that becomes possible they will be provided opportunities of part-time non-formal education.

Shift of Emphasis: The emphasis will now shift from sheer enrolment to retention and quality of education.

Decentralising Planning: Keeping in view the imbalances regarding elementary education, the process of planning will be decentralised and the teachers as well as the local community will be fully involved in this process.

Programme of Action : Operation Blackboard (O.B.)

Operation Blackboard envisages :

(1) Two reasonably large rooms that are usable in all weathers,

(2) Necessary toys and games material.

(3) Blackboards,

(4) Maps,

(5) Charts and

(6) Other learning materials.

Funds: Funds for the Operation Blackboard will be provided by the Government of India to the State Government on advanced reimbursement basis.

Programme of Action : The New Programme for Non-Formal Education

Use of Modern Technological Tools: Modern technological tools such as solar packs for provision of power in NFE Centres, audio-visual aids, radio-cassette players will be used to improve the learning environment of NFE Centres.

Special Features of NFE: NFE will have certain characteristics which will help in maintenance of the quality of the programme. These features include:

(1) A learner-centered approach;

(2) Emphasis on learning rather than teaching;

(3) Organisation of activities so as to enable learners to progress at their own pace;

(4) Use of efficient techniques to ensure fast pace of learning ;

(5) Stress on continuous learner-evaluation;

(6) Creation of participatory learning environment;

(7) Organisation of joyful co-curricular activities including group singing and dancing, plays and skits, games and sports, excursions, etc.;

(8) Encouragement to ensure that all facilities and incentives given to iris, children of S C/S T, and others in the formal system, are made available in the non-formal system as well in addition to provision of free textbooks and stationery to all pupils.

Appointment of Women Instructors: Wherever possible, women will be appointed as instructors.

Training of Instructors: A variety of agencies will be involved and help taken of diverse training aids and educational technology including TV andVCP/VCR.

Supervision: The work of supervision may be entrusted to wholetime IFE supervisors with about 20-25 centres under his/her charge or preferably local trained youth.

Secondary Education

Secondary Education in its Differentiated Role : Secondary education begins to expose students to the differentiated roles of science, the humanities and social sciences. This is also an appropriate stage to provide children with sense of history and national perspective and give them opportunities to understand their constitutional duties and rights as citizens. Conscious iternalisation of healthy work ethos and of the values of human and composite culture will be brought about through appropriately formulated curricula. vocationalisation through specialised institutions or through the refashioning secondary education can, at this stage, provide valuable manpower for economic growth. Access to secondary education will be widened to cover areas unserved by it at present. In other areas the main emphasis will be on consolidation.

Opportunities for Children with Special Talent: It is universally accepted that children with special talent or aptitude should be provided opportunities to proceed at a faster pace, by making good quality education available to them, irrespective of their capacity to pay for it. Pace-setting schools intended to serve this purpose will be established in various part of the country on a given pattern, but with full scope for innovation and experimentation. Their broad aims will be:

(1) to serve the objective of excellence, coupled with equity and social justice (with reservation for scheduled castes and scheduled tribes);

(2) to promote national integration by providing opportunities to talented children largely rural, from different parts of the country to live and learn together;

(3) to develop their full potential, and most importantly the schools will be residential and free of charge; and

(4) to become catalysts of a nation-wide programme of school improvement.

Programmes of Implementation. The following programmes have been proposed :

(a) By 2000, the unserved areas will be fully covered.

(b) Open schools would be established in a phased manner by 1990 to provide opportunitites for non-formal education.

(c) Adequate playground facilities, where needed, will have to be provided.

(d) A programme for construction of additional class-room and laboratoly facilities in schools.

(e) In order to replace the equipment once given, it is suggested that community participation by way of student contribution at the rate Rs. 10 to Rs. 15 per month should be levied, except for girls.

(f) The teacher's competencies would be improved by attracting better-qualified people to the profession and by improving the pre-service and in-service training programmes.

(g) There will be overall improvement in curriculum, the textual material, teaching practices and examination evaluation methods.

(h) The ratio of higher secondary to secondary schools should be 1 :3.

(i) Schools should be helped to have all the three streams with a vocational stream in selected schools.

Navodaya Vidyalayas. Under the scheme of Navodaya Vidyalayas for catering to the category of high achievers. One such vidyalaya will be set-up in each district during the Seventh Five Year Plan period.

Programme for Gifted Students: Special arrangements for gifted students will be made on modular basis for every small group of students in a small number of subjects of interest to them.

Vocationalisation of Secondary Education

Recommendations

The new policy observes that the introduction of systematic, well-planned and rigorously implemented programmes of vocational education is crucial in the proposed educational reorganisation. These elements are meant to enhance individual employability, to reduce the mis-match between the demand and supply of skilled man-power, and to provide an alternative for those pursuing higher education without particular interest or purpose.

A Distinct Stream: Vocational education will be a distinct stream, intended to prepare students for identified occupations spanning several areas of activity. These courses will ordinarily be provided after the secondary stage, but keeping the scheme flexible, they may also be made available after Class VIII.

Health Planning and Health Service Management: Health planning and health service management should optimally interlock with the education and training of appropriate categories of health manpower through health-related vocational courses. Health education at the primary and middle level will ensure the commitment of the individual to family and community health, and lead to health-related vocational courses at the +2 stage of higher secondary education. Efforts will be made to devise similar vocational courses based on agriculture, marketing, social services, etc.

Dual Responsibility. The establishment of vocational courses or institutions will be the responsibility of the Government as well as employers in the public and private sectors. Appropriate programmes will also be started for the handicapped.

Opportunities of Professional Growth through Bridge Courses. Graduates of vocational courses will be given opportunities, under determined conditions, for professional growth, career improvement and lateral entry into courses of general, technical and professional education through appropriate bridge courses.

Programmes for Neo-literates: Non-formal, flexible and need-based vocational programmes will also be made available to neoliterates, youth who have completed primary education, school dropouts, persons engaged in work and unemployed or partially employed persons. Special attention in this regard will be given to women.

Coverage. It is proposed that vocational courses cover 10 per cent of higher secondary students by 1990 and 25 per cent, by 1995. Steps will be taken to see that a substantial majority of the products of vocational courses are employed or become self-employed.

Management of Vocational Education. Keeping in view the variety of functions to be performed in planning and implementing programmes of vocational education and the scale of operations commensurate with the desired changes at post-primary, post-secondary and post-higher secondary stages, it is necessary to organise an effective management system.

Programme of Action

Four areas of Vocational Programme

The four key result areas for ensuring logical development of the programme of action include:

(1) Development of the system and its management.

(2) Vocational education programmes.

(3) Programmes for special groups out of school population.

(4) Targets and preparation for development.

Development of the System

Developing organisational structure includes the following:

(a) A Joint Council for Vocational Education (JCVE), to be set up by the ' MHRD (Ministry of Human Resource Development), will be the apex body for policy-planning and co-ordination of vocational education at nation level. In addition, a Bureau of Vocational Education will be established in the Ministry of Human Resource Development.

(b) A Central Institute of Vocational Education (CIVE) under the NCERT will be set up to perform research and development, monitoring and evaluation functions.

(c) State Governments will set up appropriate bodies/organisations like States Council of Vocational Education (SCVE), State Institute of Vocational Education (SIVE), etc.

(d) Organisations like NCERT, CIVE, Regional Colleges of Education (RCEs), SCERTs, SIVEs, Technical Teachers Training institutes (TTTIs),. etc. will be strengthened.

(e) State Councils of Vocational Education will organise district wise needs assessment of Vocational manpower, through area vocational surveys.

(f) State Departments of Vocational Education will give directives and guidelines to vocational institutions to develop linkages between schools, employers and voluntary organisations in the community, to facilitates successful implementation of vocational programmes ensuring optimum resource utilisation as well as effectiveness.

Vocational Education Programmes

(a) Vocational programmes for 8+ students will be introduced on experimental basis on a limited scale in different States by State Departments of Vocational Education.

(b) Programme at 10+ level will be formulated by SCERT/SIVEs in the light of guidelines laid down by NCERT. The SCVEs shall facilitate the introduction of these programmes on the basis of result of area vocational surveys in selected in a phased manner keeping in view the national targets.

(c) To provide more opportunities to students for 10+ vocational course in engineering and technology, 100 more vocational institutions shall be established.

(d) JCVE will provide in a phased manner to 70% of the higher secondary-vocational stream graduates stipend to undergo paid apprenticeship in appropriate industries.

(e) Tertiary level programmes like diploma in Vocational subjects, Advanced Diploma programmes and Degree programmes will be introduced in selected polytechnics, affiliated colleges and universities, as well as in special institutes set up for this purpose.

(f) Entrepreneurs/self-employment skills will be developed in vocational stream students, through curriculum, special training programmes as well as paid apprenticeship facilities.

(g) State Departments of Vocational Education and SCVEs will formulate necessary schemes for the purpose.

(h) State Directorates of Vocational Education will set up Career Guidance Cells at district level.

(i) NCERT/CIVE, SCERTs/SIVEs, RCEs, CDC, TTTIs and other institutes will develop bridge/transfer courses in accordance with the guidelines laid down by JVCE. Suitable schemes for course offering shall be developed by SCVEs.

Programme or Special Groups and Out of School Population

Involvement of Public/Private Sector:

(1) JCVE will evolve scheme to involve the public/private sector industry in vocational education through appropriate incentives/rewards.

(2) JCVE/SCVEs/State Departments of Vocational Education will identify and support voluntary organisations engaged in the vocational education of special groups like women, tribals, handicapped and disabled, etc. Suitable scheme for this will be formulated by JCVE.

Non-Formal Programme:

(1) All polytechnic institutions, ITS, other vocational and technical training institutions, selected higher secondary schools, colleges and special institutes will engage themselves in imparting vocational education through non-formal programmes to the rural and non-organised sector in a phased manner. Suitable schemes for the purpose, like the Community Polytechnic Scheme, will be formulated by JCVE for respective categories of institution.

(2) Selected Engineering Colleges, Polytechnics, Industrial Training Institutes and other Vocational and Technical Training Schools/Institutes will engage themselves in conducting part-time vocational courses for the benefit of special groups and those already employed.

Setting up Special Institutes:

(1) Special vocational training institutes for women, tribals and other weaker section of the society to meet identified needs, will be established by the State Departments of Vocational Education.

(2) Centres for vocational training of the handicapped will be set up in institutions like special institutes of relevant/useful technology. Distinct Vocational Training Centres, 1TIs and Polytechnics to equip this section of the society with appropriate employable skills.

Targets and Preparation for Development

Targets. For 10 % diversion by 1990, provision will have to be made for 2.5 lakhs students In view to the action already taken, additional requirements for 2.5 lakhs students can be met by marginal expansion of the infra-structure and resources but for 25 % diversion by 1995 advance action will have to be taken by the States and Central Government in terms of building a requisite level of insfrastructure and facilities.

Teacher Training. A phased and co-ordinated programme for the training of teachers, principals and key officials in the vocational education system using the available infrastructures in organisations like NCERT, RCEs, SIVEs, TTTIs, CDC, State Institutes of Education, will be undertaken. Scheme will be drawn up by concerned institutions in accordance with guidelines given by JCVE. Crash programmes will also be organised by concerned institutions to meet the immediate area requirements for which a scheme shall be formulated by JCVE.

Review. NCERT/CIVE and SCERT/SIVE will formulate schemes for the review of vocational programmes-in accordance with the guidelines laid down by JCVE.

Teacher Elementary and Secondary Levels

Recommendations

Continuing Education: Teachers will continue to play a crucial role in he formulation and implementation of educational programmes. It has been observed in the draft of the new National Policy on Education that teacher education is a continuous process. Its pre-service and in-service components are inseparable. As the first step, the system of teacher education will be overhauled.

The new programme of teacher-education will emphasize continuing education and the end for teacher to meet the themes envisaged in this policy.

DIET AND NCTE : District Institutes of Education and Training (DIET) will be established with the capability to organise pre-service service courses for elementary school teachers and for the personnel working in non-formal and adult education. As DIETs get established, sub-standard institutions will be phased out. Selected Secondary/Teacher Training college will be upgraded to complement the work of State Councils of Educational Research and Training. The National Council for Teacher Education will be provided the necessary resources and capability to accredited institutions of teacher education and provide guidance regarding curricula and methods. Networking arrangements will be created between institutions of education and University Department of Education.

Programme of Action

Implementation Strategies

Operationalisation of implementation strategies will call for strong determination, meticulous planning, innovative and participatory method of programme implementation and a considerable amount of financial resources.

The programme of action includes following implementation strategics and operational pre-requisites;

1. Introduction of reforms in the system of selection of teachers.
2. Improvement in the living the working/service conditions of teachers.
3. Creation of an effective machineiy for removal of grievances.
4. Involvement of teachers in the planning and management of education.
5. Involvement of Teacher's Associations in upholding the dignity of teachers, their professional integrity and curbing professional misconduct.
6. Preparation of a code of professional ethics for teachers and assuring that teachers perform their duties in accordance with acceptable norms.
7. Willingness to take hard decision with regard to selection to teachers and code of conduct for teachers.
8. Creation of opportunities and an atmosphere to promote autonomy and innovation among teachers.

Teacher Status

Living and Working Conditions of Teachers: The most important factor affecting the status of teachers is their living and working conditions. Some of the directions in which action will be taken are given below :

Pay and Allowances: The movement shall be providing pay and allowances to teachers at all levels which are keeping with their educational status in society. The anomaly of providing lower scales of pay to some categories of teachers (e.g., teachers of physical education, fine arts and craft teachers) and librarians will be done away with.

Professional Growth: It is intended to link career advancement with professional growth. The data based comprehensive appraisal would, therefore, be necessary it suitable intervals.

Retirement and Old-age Benefits and Medical Care: All teachers will be eligible for retirement and medical benefits identical with Government servants.

Housing: Special measures will be taken to provide housing facilities for teachers in uiban as well as rural areas. Variety of .nancial resources will be used for construction of houses in desert, hilly, tribal and remote rural areas.

Study Leave: All teachers will be entitled on full pay, one long-term study leave.

Special Provision for Women Teachers: All women teachers desirous of being posted with their spouses will be posted as such provided that the latter are working in desert, hilly, tribal or remote rural areas. Placement of women teachers will be made keeping in view their domestic obligations.

Uniformity of Service Conditions: It is desirable that there should be uniformity of service conditions for all teachers. Specific directions in this respect would be worked out in consolation with State Governments.

Posting and Transfer of Teachers: It is essential that postings and transfer of teachers are made in accordance with certain norms. By and large, a teacher should not be moved for three years after his first appointment.

National Foundation for Teacher Welfare: The activities of the foundation will be enlarged, the eligibility of teachers will be widened and necessary organisational support will be provided to make the Foundation an effective instrument of teacher's welfare.

Teacher's Paticipation: It is only through their active participation at all levels of management that the principle responsibility of educational transformation can be entrusted to the teachers. The main features of teacher's participation would be as follows :

(a) Involvement of teachers in implementation of NPE.

(b) Participation of teachers in the policy making and management forms such as CABE, SABE, etc.

(c) Provision of Executive Committee/Syndicate and Academic Council level consultative bodies with teachers.

Teacher's Associations: Strong, unified and responsible teacher's assoications are necessary for the protection of the dignity and rights of teacher as also for ensuring proper professional conduct of teachers. It would be advisable to encourage development of such associations. It is necessary to stress the need for democratic functioning of all these organisations in the absence of which they tend to break into small groups and their credibility and capacity to serve the suffers.

Recruitment of Teachers: Methods of recruitment of teachers will be reorganised to ensure objectivity, merit and conformity with spatial and functional requirements. Discussions will soon be intiated with State Government and agencies such as the UGC/ AICTE, etc. to evolve such a method of recruitment. The need to reduce ad hoc and temporary appointments and fill vacancies specially will be kept in view.

Every effort will be made to make teaching an attractive profession to which persons of talent and commitment may feel motivated to join. Apart from improvement in working and living conditions, the procedures of selection of teachers will also be reorganised. Persons who have given evidence of interest in teaching, love for children, a spirit of adventure and creativity, and commitment for social upliftment will be preferred.

In the school system, particularly at the elementary level, the desert, hilly, tribal and remote rural areas have always had difficulty in regard to placement of teachers. A systematic and phased programme will be prepared to deal with this problem.

Keeping in view the importance of non-formal education in universalisation of elementary education and of adult education in the strategy of educational development evisaged in NPE, special arrangements will be made for training of instructors.

Teacher Education

1. District Institute of Education and Training (DIET) and National Council for Teacher Education (NCTE). Professional training of teachers to be employed in elementary and secondary schools is a pre-requisite in'all parts of the country. The requirement is waived only in areas or among groups where there is a severe shortage of teachers. A large number of these institutions suffer from inadequate facilities (human, physical and academic) to provide good professional education. Curricula remain unrevised for years.

Keeping in view the central place of teacher education, NPW calls for its overhaul as the first step towards educational reorganisation. Giving specific importance to the training of elementary school teachers, it is envisaged that selected institutions would be developed as District Institutes of Education and Training (DIET), both for pre-service and in-service course of elementary school teachers and for continued education of the personnel working in non-formal and adult education programme. Reorganisation of secondary teacher education system is also implied in the policy.

The National Council for Teacher Education will be given the statutory status and necessary resources to play its role.

Functions of Elementary Teacher Education Institutions. An important change in the educational system will be brought about by the radical transformation of the present system of Elementary Teacher Education.

The functions of an Elementary Teacher Education Institutions would include:

(1) Pre-service and in-service education of teachers for the formal school system.

(2) Continuing education of Non-formal and Adult Education Instructors and Supervisors.

(3) Training and orientation of heads in planning and management.

(4) Orientation of community leaders, functionaries of voluntary organisation and others influencing school-level education.

(5) Academic support to school complexes and District Boards of Education.

(6) Action research and experimentation work.

(7) Serving as evaluation centre for primary and upper primary schools as well as non-formal and adult education programme.

(8) Provision of services of resource and learning centres for teacnei s and instructors.

(9) Consultancy and advice.

(10) Each State Government will set-up immediately a Task Force for making as assessment of the number of institutions of this nature required in the State, keeping in view the various relevant Programmes of Action.

(11) The DIET will perfom all the functions mentioned in the preceding points. The NFE/Adult Education/ District Resource Units would be an integral part of DIET for which additional faculty will be provided.

(12) Latest technology as computer-based learning, VCR, TV, etc. will be provided at DIETs. The teachers receiving training at DIETs would be encouraged to develop their own programmes using the facilities available at DIETs and to use these materials as instructional resources. Capability for making copies of video cassettes, audio cassettes, etc. would also be provided to these institutes. Imaginative use of traditional teaching aids would be emphasized and teachers will be encouraged to improvise their own instructional materials.

Secondary Teacher Education: The responsibilty for secondary teacher education would continue to rest with Colleges of Teacher Education affiliated to Universities. The University, in co-operation with NCTE, will exercise responsibility for academic aspects. These institutions would also be responsible for continuing education programmes or secondary school teachers. Some Colleges of Teacher Education will be developed as comprehensive institutions organising programmes for primary teacher education and possibly also, four-year integrated courses after higher secondary stage, in addition to the usual B.Ed./M.Ed. coures. In order to promote innovations and experimentation, good Colleges and Departments of Education of Universities will also be given autonomous status.

In-service Education of Teachers: A great deal of responsibility would be given to SCERTs. They would have the major role of planning, sponsoring, monitoring and evaluation of the in-service education programme for all levels of teachers, instructors and other educational personnel. The need of in-service education of teachers is there because of changing national goals, vision of school curricula, additional inputs in teaching-learning system, inadequate background of teachers, etc. The State level agency would take cognizance of all the needs before preparing a programme of in-service education for a given period of time.

SCERTs would also prepare suitable material for in-service education of teachers, undertake orientation of key persons, monitoring and evolution of programmes. Similar steps for training of teachers in vocational, stream should also be taken by SCERTs.

The District Institutes of Education and Training for the primary level would be the major agency to conduct the programmes of in-service education for primary teachers. Assistance would be sought from school complexes in the district. In the case of secondary school teachers, the progmramme would be extended through teacher training institutes and the centres for continuing education.

All in-service education programmes cannot be organised in face-to-face modality especially in view of the numbers involved. Distance in-service education will be prepared and extended with the help of broadcasting agencies. SCERTs would be equipped with necessary resources of production of learning material other than print.

The NCERT, SCERT in cooperation with NCTE (National Council For Teacher Education) will continue to perform the function of preparing learning material orientation of senior teachers, educators etc.

QUESTIONS

1. Comment upon major features of NPE-1986.
2. Discuss briefly elementary education and early childhood care in the context of NPE-1986.
3. Discuss implementation strategies, operation blackboard and programme for non-formal education for elementary education in the light of Programme of Action.
4. Describe briefly secondary education with reference of NPE-1986.
5. Write briefly on vocationalisation of education in the context of NPE-1986.
6. Describe briefly regarding teacher education in India in the light of NPE-1986.

9

Revised Policy

Later, under P.V. Narasimha Rao, the National Policy on Education was revised in the light of specific guidelines e.g. equity as social justice, decentralisation of educational management development of human society and empowerment for work. The Review Committee (also known as Rama Murti Review Committee-1992) reviewed NPE-1986 and recommended on certain aspects with the given guideline. The recommendations were given on aspects like equity, social justice and education ; early childhood case and education; adult and continuing education ; education and right to work ; higher education ; technical and management education ; resources of education. The present chapter briefly deals with all these aspects.

Guiding Principles for Review

The approach of Ramamurti Review Committee (1992) in reviewing the National Policy on Education-1986 and its implementation was guided by the following principal concerns :

1. Equity and social justice.
2. Decentralisation of educational management at all levels.
3. Establishment of a participative educational order.
4. Inculcation of values indispensable for creation of an enlightened and human society.
5. Empowerment for work.
6. Human being is to be valued as more than a resource.

Equity, Social Justice and Education

Women Education

Review Committee recommended that the schooling of girls in villages must be linked with the need of easy access to water, fuel and fodder. This can be helpful in programmes on forestry, drinking water and greening of common lands.

Priority should be given to those habitations/villages where enrolment and retention rate for girls in schools is below the average rate at the state level. Planning for educational development should be done at the block level or sub-block level. Educational complexes are proposed. Information will be provided here by teachers, Anganwadi workers, village level functionaries, representatives of women groups and community level workers.

Early Childhood Care Education (ECCE)

(1) ECCE services should be provided in proximity to every primary and middle school. This should be linked with elementary education.

(2) Priority should be given to programme for 0-3 age group, particularly to under-privileged sections of society.

(3) The ECCE centres should include school hours so that girls in age group 6-14 are relieved of responsibility of sibling care.

(4) The management of the ECCE centres and Anganwadis should be decentralised. It should be participative.

Regional Disparities

(1) Problem of regional disparities should be taken into consideration while designing programmes for universalisation of primary education for girls.

(2) Priority should be given to educational status of women in the educationally backward districts.

(3) Eucational planning should be done at the educational complexes.

(4) Dencentralised and participative approach in planning and management should be followed.

Curriculum

Curriculum in school should include :

(1) Positive role of women in Indian society.

(2) Special efforts for girls for science and mathematics education.

(3) Undifferentiated curriculum for boys and girls.

(4) Such material/content which should be free from gender bias.

(5) Exclude such traditional contents which hinder the positive development of women.

(6) Legal information which may be useful to women and children in their protection.

(7) Steps for improving involvement of girls in physical education and sports.

Textbooks

Textbooks at the school level as well as university level should eliminate the invisibility of women and gender bias.

Media

(a) Media should contribute to promote gender equality and empowerment of women.

(b) Advertisments using women as sex symbols must be dealt with seriously.

(c) Media should highlight the positive role of women in society.

(d) Media should develop awareness about the elementary education and vocational education of women.

(e) Code of ethics in connection with women in media programmes should be evolved.

(f) A national policy on communication giving gender perspective to all forms and processes of mass communication should be formulated urgently. The National Commission on Women should play an active role in this exercise.

Vocational Education

(a) State level planning should be there for vocational education of girls/ women.

(b) Vocational education of women should be encouraged in non-traditional areas also.

(c) Vocational education of girls should be provided after 8th class. Vocational training should also be given to drop-out cases below 8th standard.

(d) Diversification of courses should be there.

(e) Stipends, fellowships, placement, craft-education etc. should be the part of vocational education.

Training of Teachers and Other Educational Personnel

(a) Teacher training programmes should be evaluated and the programmes must be restructured keeping in view women education. Problems of girl/women education should be taken into account.

(b) Decentralisation in curriculum planning, development and implementation is needed.

(c) Curriculum planning, development and implementation should be joint effort of DBETs, Educational Complexes, Women's study centres, educators and grassroot level organisations.

(d) Restructured curriculum should be implemented and teacher educators should be trained through in-service programmes.

(e) In-service programmes for school teachers must be organised by DIETs in consultation with Educational Complexes.

(f) Administrators and planners should be sensitised to the problems of women.

Research and Development of Women Studies

(a) Women's study centres should be organised in universities and social science research institutions within the Eighth Plan.

(b) Research findings of these centres should be consulted in the curriculum planning and development.

Women Studies Courses

(a) Women studies courses should be introduced at the undergraduate level.

(b) Problems of women should be adequately covered in the courses.

(c) Experts from different women centres and organisations should be involved in curriculum development.

Extension Services

Women studies should be extended to colleges and other higher education institutions.

Representation of Women of Educational Hierarchy

(a) Women teachers in schools (Primary, Middle and High) should be at least 50 per cent. Preference in selection should be given to women teachers living within or near the habitation.

(b) Accommodation must be provided on priority basis to women.

(c) Promotional avenues for women should be there in the educational hierarchy. Women should be represented in decision-making bodies in teaching and educational administration.

(d) Women should be involved in framing recruitment/service procedures, guidelines for promotion etc.

Empowerment of Women

(a) Development at the district or block level ofMahila Samakhya having decision-making powers.

(b) Mahila Samakhya will have link with Early Child Care Centres and this body will also make efforts for universalisation of girl's elementary education.

(c) Issues like economic independence, health including reproductive health and sexually should be taken care to for the empowerment of women.

Adult Education

Mahila Samakhya should work for adult education of women. This will help in women empowerment.

Resources

Allocations of funds should be earmarked for girls at all levels. 50 per cent allocation is needed for girls at the elementary level. Special allocation is needed under allocation for SC/ST.

Management

(a) Schemes for women related to decentralisation and participative management should be continued.

(b) Educational complexes under Panchayati Raj framework should plan, implement and monitor women education programmes.

(c) Head of institutions should be made responsible for planning and universalisation of girl's education.

Scheduled Castes, Scheduled Tribes and Backward Classes

Incentive Schemes

(a) Studies should be conducted on the impact of incentives provided to girls for retention and enrolment of SC/ST children in schools.

(b) Profiles should be prepared for educationally backward communities.

(c) Educational programmes should be developed on the basis of research findings.

Status of Access of Education

Habitations dominated by SC/ST are still there where schools are not there within walking distance. Steps are needed to be taken in this direction.

Improvement of Capability and Educational Environment

(1) Remedial teaching should be organised throughout the session.

(2) Enrichment of learning environment should be done through efforts.

(3) School linked libraries should be there in backward areas including SC/ST habitations. Bicycle-borne mobile libraries should be provided regional languages should be used in the literature.

(4) Different subjects and co-curricular activities should be identified in the light of talents and aptitudes of students.

(5) Workshops/work-camps should be organised.

(6) Curriculum for educationally backward children should include the following :

* Science and Mathematics.
* Expression (oral and written) and creative writing.
* History and Sociology of SC/ST and Backward classes.
* Contribution of SC/ST/Backward Classes to the development of the nation.
* Role of Women (ST/SC/Backward Classes) in national development.

Recruitment of SC/ST Teachers

Ensure that SC/ST teachers recruited in schools (Govt. & Govt. aided) are 15% and 7% respectively.

Curriculum and Tribal Culture

Core curriculum should include rich diversity and cultural aspects of tribes.

Special Component Plan and Tribal Sub-plan Schemes

Special Component Plan and Tribal Sub-plan Schemes should be developed under special component plan and tribal sub-plan.

Intensive Area Approach

Ministry of welfare should provide list of SC/ST habitations and blocks so that implementation of various programmes for them may be properly coordinated by the Ministry.

Monitoring

An agency in each State must be there to report development to the Central Government.

Education of Minorities

1. A machinery should be set up for the purpose of monitoring the State Government regarding grant of recognition to schools managed by minorities.
2. Programmes already prepared should be implemented. Programmes for community polytechnics should be completed in the remaining 25 districts in the Eighth Five Year Plan.
3. Principals/managers/teachers of minority managed schools should be given orientation by SCERT/DIET/CTE/IASE at state level.
4. IGNOU should establish distance education centres for minorities.

Education of Handicapped

(a) Awareness should be developed among people about various aspects of handicapped persons.

(b) Family of a handicapped person should be provided incentives and training.

(c) Parent's group/community groups should be formed.

(d) Flexibility should be there for the education of handicapped, special schools may be opened for those who cannot be educated in normal schools.

(e) Education should be provided through formal, non-formal and informal means.

(f) Vocational training for boys and girls should be arranged. Schools should be opened for this purpose.

(g) Books should be developed using Bharati Braille (developed by National Insitute of Visually Handicapped).

(h) Efforts in work for Braille nations in Mathematics and Science are required.

(i) Special curricular programmes should be developed for moderately mentally retarded.

(j) Pre-service teacher education colleges should be established. Special courses should be the part of normal B.Ed. courses.

(k) Atleast one resource faculty should be there in DIET.

(l) Learning resources like Braillex produced by Federal Republic of Germany should be arranged. It consists of cassettes and printing conversion devices like "tactacon". Aids for visually handicapped should be reviewed and disseminated.

(m) Research should be done further to know the needs of handicapped persons.

Common School System

(a) Common school system is the first step in securing equity and social justice in education.

(b) Increased outlay for elementary education should be used for provision of infrastructure and quality education in the Government schools, local body and aided schools and thus these schools should be converted into neighbourhood schools.

(c) Special allocation should be made for schools for backward areas, slums, tribal areas, desert, marshy places, drought areas, flood prone areas, coastal belts and islands.

(d) Use of mother tongue should be encouraged.

(e) Implementation of Common School System should be implemented within 10 years.

(f) Ways should be explored to include expensive schools in this scheme.

Navodaya Vidyalaya

The Committee recommended following alternatives for Navodaya Vidyalayas:

1. No further Navodaya Vidyala will be opened. The existing Navodaya Vidayalaya Scheme may be reviewed at the end of 1992-93.

2. The Navodaya schools should be run by state Government as residential centres.

3. The Navodaya Vidayala Scheme may be transformed into Navodaya Vidyalaya Programme of broad talent nurturing and pace setting. A day school under the common school system can function in the premises of the Navodaya Vidyalayas.

Early Childhood Care and Education (ECCE)

1. Scope of Article 45 of the Constitution should be enlarged to include early childhood care and education (ECCE).
2. ECCE should be included in the minimum needs programme.
3. The Department of Women and Child Development in the Ministry of HRD at the centre and the Departments of Social Welfare in the States should be acountable for implementation of ECCE.
4. Principles of diversity, flexibility and decentralised management and funding should be followed. If possible ECCE centre should be linked with primary school.
5. ICDS should become a participatory network of decentralised ECCE centres.
6. Curriculum development should be on the basis of local needs. Formal teaching models should be discouraged.
7. The details regarding personnel and training in POA should be implemented immediately e.g., remuneration, motivation, training, social status, job satisfaction etc. need immediate attention. Education Department (Centre and State) should take the reponsibility of teacher-education. DIETs should contribute to teacher education. Educational complexes should coordinate with DIETs.
8. Modular approach should be followed. Holistic goals should be achieved with local need based curriculum. Child-centred and non-formal education should be organised at this stage.
9. Accreditation of the training programme should be done.

10. Vocational education of ECCE at +2 level should be there. Feasibility of such vocational programme after 8th class should also be explored.
11. ICDS and other centrally sponsored schemes for ECCE should be shifted to States/UTs.
12. Management of Anganwadis and other ECCE Centres should be fully handed over to voluntary organisations and local community groups through Panchayati Raj or framewoik.
13. Local bodies should constitute village level or mohalla level committees having representatives from Anganwadi workers for the purpose of planning, coordinating and monitoring of ECCE centre. Educational complex should develop plans for ECCE and arrange training through DIET.
14. ECCE should be accountable to community.
15. State Government should ensure funding provide guidelines, facilitate training through SCERT/DIET, provision of materials, coordination, monitoring and development of public awareness.
16. A central fund for child care should be set up at the centre level.
17. A 10 year action and resource allocation plan for building national network of child care should be prepared. 70% of children below six years would be covered by a package of services by 2000 A.D. as suggested by POA.
18. Funds may be drawn from Government, local bodies, parents and donations. Special allocation of 100 crores should be done initially.

Universalisation of Elementary Education

Right to Education. The right to education should be examined for inclusion amon; fundamental rights guaranteed under the Constitution of India.

Thrust Areas. Following three thrust areas should be incorporated:

(a) Convergence of services

(b) Linkage between the school and the community

(c) Decentralised and participative mode of educational planning and management.

Child Centred Approach. Child-centred approach to education was appreciated by the Review Committee. Joy, fun, exploration and play should be integral part of learning in the early stages of primary education. These elements are not being emphasized in the educational practice today. The role of singing, drawing, clay-modelling, games, folk-art and folk-love should be emphasised for enriching the learning process.

Remedial Teaching. Committee is not clear why remedial instruction is restricted to first generation learning in NPE.

Cognitive, Affective and Psychmotor Objectives. Cognitive and psychomotor objectives have been emphasized with the growth on the child. There is need to emphasize affective domain objectives and psycho-motor objectives at the early stages of the child.

No Retention. The Committee endorses the declaration in NPE that there should be no detention at the primary stage. Non-retention at the primary stage should be presented in the policy as a positive concept of continuous, disaggregated and comprehensive evaluation as a means of improving the quality of learning with a clear understanding that the concept of a terminal examination has no place in child-centred education.

No Corporal Punishment. The policy declares that corporal punishment will be firmly excluded. There was need to mention measures to control the socio-cultural, psychological and educational factors that justify corporal punishment in the minds of the teachers.

Timings. NPE should have spelt out reasons which may justify the non-adjustment of tunings of the school and vacations as per the convenience of children.

Quality of Education. Stress should be given to the role of the teacher, the community and the social environment as important factors in the improvement of qualify of school education.

Improvement in Enrolment and Retention. Data regarding enrolment is not reliable and hence policy must stress on improvement both on enrolment and retention.

Curriculum. +2 curriculum should not be allowed to determine curriculum of primary and middle schools. The curriculum for primary and middle stages should aim at evolving a self-sufficient model of knowledge, skills and attitudes so that students who may not go for +2 stage may enter the world of work and continue to learn through self-learning strategies.

Integration of Formal and Non-Formal Education. Integrate formal and non-formal education systems over a period of time so that their cadres, infrastructure and management structures would form an organic whole.

Non-Formalising the Formal School. The Committee recommends that formal school should be non-formalised over a period of time by taking following steps :

(a) Shifting school timings to early morning hours, afternoons or late evening as per convenience of children. Village Education Committee and Educational Complex must be consulted before making these changes.

(b) School calender should be adjustmen in accordance with agricultural activities, local cultural programmes and weekly markets. This will be good for optimising school attendance.

(c) Chid-centred approach should be introduced. School time can be reduced but learning hours can be increased by using pedagogic strategies like inquiry, play-way activities, creative writing, peer group learning, experimentation etc. Pedagogic pratices can be enriched through creative use of singing, drawing, story-telling, folk-arts, and folk-lores.

(d) Link must be kept with at least one day-care centre. Anganwadi workers should be viewed as associates of the staff.

(e) Hold classes twice a day wherever possible. Mornings should be used for written work and evening for oral work, games and cultural programmes.

(f) Introduce "ungraded classroom" and encourage all children at different levels to learn at their own pace.

(g) Content and process of learning should be related to life of community and environment.

(h) Allow working children, especially girls, to drop-in the school at any time of the school or the year. Migration cases from other villages/habitations/ towns should be allowed. This flexibility will be possible in case we follow ungraded classroom approach.

(i) Teacher-education and placement of teachers will have to be restructured in case we want to non-formalise the formal education adopting ways mentioned above. Some points are listed below :

* Head of the school should be empowered to recruit para-teachers *(Shiksha Karmis)* for early morning or evening classes besides regular staff.
* The emoluments of para-staff should be respectable.
* Selection of para-staff should preferably be from local community. Qualification may be even less.
* Para-staff may be recruited as regular staff.
* Training of para-staff must be organised.

(j) Following measures should be adopted as pre-condition for non-formalising the formal schools:

* Appointments, promotion and posting of teachers should be through a management system involving school. Village Education Committee and Educational Complex.
* Local Community should be empowered to monitor and support the school.
* School should be developed into a community school which should take interest in social and cultural life of the village.
* Modern teaching aids should be introduced.

Operation Blackboard. Comittee recommends the following:

(a) The State Government should devolve all decision-making powers concerning Operation Blackboard to Educational Complexes. Educational Complexes will consult DIETs, concerned school and Village Education Committees.

(b) The schools and Village Education Committees will be fully responsible for universahsation of elementary education. They will plan and execute plans for Operation Blackboard.

(c) Operation Blackboard should be given the status of one of the priorities for univ2ersalisation of elementary education.

(d) Women teacher should be selected from local community. They should be given accomodation, security and other support services.

Measures to "Reach Out" to Children

(a) Provide at least one primary school to each habitation with a population of 300 or more upto 2000 A.D. For the time being para-teacher attached with nearest-school should serve such villages.

(b) Provide one middle school for each habitation with a population of 500 or more. Para-teachers should be provided for the time being.

(c) Para-schools should serve the habitation with less than 300 population by the end of Eighth Five Year Plan.

(d) Emphasis should be given to keep the enrolment and retention rate of girls above the average rate of the State.

(e) Para-schools should be arranged in the morning, afternoon or late in the evening for those children who are engaged in work at home or somewhere else.

(f) Strategies and Measures for Achieving Universalisation of Elementary Education.

The Review Committee recommended the following for achieving universalisation of elementary education :

(a) Each school should be fully responsible and accountable for formulating and implementing strategies for universalisation of elementary education in the area under its coverage, strategies may be adult education, para-schools, operation blackboard.

(b) Head of the school should be authorised to appoint para-teachers (Shiksha-Karmcharis).

(c) Teacher must be encouraged to develop child-centred models of education in the light of local needs.

(d) Vocationalisation must be emphasized up to 8th class.

(e) Goal of universalisation of education should be viewed in two phases:

* First phase: Universalisation of Primary Education

* Second Phase : Universalisation of Elementary Education

(f) Principle of differentiated or disaggregated targets and pluralistic educational strategies should be adopted for universlisation of elementary education.

(g) Management should be decentralised and participatory. (S) Monitoring should be at three levels in a coordinated manner: school level, district level and state level.

(h) Monthly or yearly functions of community for collective evaluation.

Adult and Continuing Education

Review Committee recommended the following :

1. Needs of Adults

(a) Adult education should take into account development needs of adults e.g., employment, housing, nutrition and health.

(b) Awareness about fundamental rights, basic laws, secularism and democracy.

(c) Literacy needs of adults must be fulfilled.

(d) We should start with essential needs of adults followed by literacy needs.

2. Mass Compaign Strategy and Mahila Samakhya Model

(a) Mass compaign strategy should be tried further.

(b) Mahila Samakhya model should be closely monitored.

(c) Both strategies should be evaluated for taking f -ther steps.

3. Voluntrary Efforts. Voluntary agencies, community groups, political parties etc. should be encouraged for making voluntary efforts towards adult and continuing education.

4. Imparting Vocational Skills

(a) Vocational skill. should be developed in adult illiterates through the efforts of the Department of Education and Department of Rural Development and Ministry of Labour Programme like TRYSEM (training of Youth for Self-Employment) should be funded.

(b) Community polytechnics should contribute to developing vocational skills in adults.

(c) Training in various vocations will increase their chances of employment.

5. **Continuing Interface with Literacy.** Efforts should be made to keep neo-literates in interface with learning environment.

Education and Right to Work

1. **Vocationalisation of Education.** State Governments should be asked to furnish deadlines for undertaking different activities for implementing vocational education. The actitivies are production of teaching/learning materials; formulation and modification of curriculum/syllabus; completion of civic construction work; procurement of equipment; man power including teachers.

2. Work Experience/Socially Useful Productive Work/Work experience/Socially Useful productive work should be integrally linked with various subjects both at the level of contents and pedagogy.

3. **Integrated Design of Vocational Education.** An integrated design of vocational education for classes 9th to 12th should be established.

4. Structural Changes in Secondary Education

(a) Changes in secondary education are needed to make vocational education successful at the secondary level.

(b) Modular courses and credit accumulation system are to be followed.

(c) Provision of multiple exit and entry points should be provided.

(d) Vocational courses should be provided in combination with subjects as languages. Mathematics, Sciences and Social Studies.

(e) Bridge courses should be provided for having higher education.

(f) Distance learning vocational education courses should be offered both at the school level and university level.

5. Vocational Programme in Non-Formal Education Vocational programmes should be organised in non-formal system e.g., Community polytechnics and TRYSEM. This will be useful to those who do not go for formal secondary education.

6. Access to Girls/SC/ST in Vocational Courses Girls/SC/ST should get access to vocational courses. Gender bias should not come in the way.

7. **Work Benches and Practice Schools.** Theory and practice both have their own place in vocational education. For practice purpose "work benches" and "practice schools" should be identified, accredited and involved.

Work-benches and practice schools are the work situation which provide direct experiences to students within production units or developmental activities of the official agencies.

Practice school is a more institutionalised arrangement with larger units in the organised sector.

Work-bench can be carved out of smaller units from the unorganised sector as well within the neighbourhood of the school.

8. **Redesigning of Teacher Education Courses.** Redesigning of teacher education courses is needed in the light of requirements of a developing society. Technologists, foremen, skilled craftmen and other trained personnel from the "world of work" should be recruited as teachers. These personnel should be given specially designed bridge courses in areas such as Psychology, Pedagogy, Evaluation, Content Planning etc.

9. **Decentralisation of Planning and Management**

(1) Decentralise management, planning and implementation to the level of individual school or school complexes as well as colleges/universities.

(2) Head of the institution and representatives of local enterprises (industry, agriculture, voluntary organisations, etc.) should take part in decision-making.

(3) Curriculum should be designed at the institution level.

(4) Manpower needs can be matched properly due to decentrali-sation.

(5) Department of Education should play only catalytic and resource-sharing roles rather directing, determining and detailing all processes.

(6) The concept of National and State Councils of Vocational Education should be re-formulated in the framework of decentralised planning, management, evaluation and accreditation.

(7) Department of Education should coordinate the agencies under Central and State Governments for establishing wages, income and employment policies.

Higher Education

Maintenance of Standards in Higher Education. Government should examine the national level statutory mechanism in the light of discouraging establishment of sub-standard colleges/ universities.

Restructuring of UGC

(1) To have effective functioning of UGC, regional offices should be opened for the purpose of decentralised disposal of problems of colleges and universities in a particular region.

(2) Adequate decentralisation of authority is needed.

(3) Restructuring of UGC is needed. There should be five full time members, apart from the chairmen and vice-chairmen, with specialisation in teaching, research, extension, management and finance.

Autonomous Colleges. Autonomous colleges should be established. Review Committee appointed by UGC should expedite the review and modalities should be evolved.

Management of Universities. Government should take a decision about the Committee regarding management of universities.

Curriculum Development. Review Committee emphasies that the process of curriculum development and designing of courses should be decentralised.

Colleges and universities should design courses on the basis of locally felt needs. Colleges and universities may seek the assistance of the UGC and their panels of experts.

Study of Revision of Pay Scale of Teacher. The UGC should conduct a study on the implementation of revised scales of University and College teachers.

Pre-Induction Training of Teachers. One-year pre-induction training should be given to teachers after their recruitment.

Research

(a) The important criteria for the choice of areas should be promise of achievement of excellence and existence of special advantages that India or Indian scholars possess.

(b) Such areas should be explored which are linked with national needs and priorities in the near or foreseeable future. Basic and applied research should be done on such areas.

(c) In certain research areas, selected institutions should be identified where research on these areas should be pursued at the advanced level. Such centres must be well-publicised and well-equipped with the aim that best of the talent knows about the challenges and opportuntiites available to them.

(d) Research groups should be established around outstanding scientists and engineers at these centres.

(e) Department of Education and UGC and other agencies should give support to these centres for research.

(f) Workers in Universities who work together with workers in these centres and who are in vicinity to these centres should be provided facilities of national laboratories in the universities.

(g) Science and technology agencies must support universities not in the form of time-bound research projects but in the setting up of sophisticated reasearch facilities in educational institutions and providing such other infrastructure facilities which will attract the best minds from all over the country. Science and technology agencies should provide certain proportion of overhead (say 20%) so that required infrastructure for research may be established with the help of this proportion of overhead.

(h) Reserach in humanities and social sciences should be directed towards contemporary realities in the country. There is a need to initiate research which takes the Indian intellectual and cultural traditions seriously, with the aim to learn from them in order to understand ourselves and to develop the composite culture of India envisaged in the Constitution.

(i) A few institutions should be selected to provide quality undergraduate education in sciences and humanities.

Extension in Universities

(a) Universities should involve themselves in development issues in the concerned regions. They should become instruments of development in the respective regions. Keeping in view, changes should be done in curriculum e.g., improvement of rural school as an extension activity.

(b) Teachers should look upon their work as of social relevance.

National Testing Service

(a) There should be National Testing Service. This will develop model tests, their administration, scoring procedure etc.

(b) The employers or educational institutions or any user agency can use these testing models keeping in view their needs.

Rural Universities. Review Committee agrees with the proposal of rural universities and institutions. The State Councils, even as envisaged in Programme of Action (POA), are to advise to the UGC in respect of maintenance of standards.

The Committee recommends the following:

(a) Ensuring autonomy in developing courses, research programmes and extension activities.

(b) Ensuring equivalence of diplomas of rural universities to degrees of universities.

(c) Coordination of extension activities.

(d) Helping in affiliation with universities/agricultural universities.

Agricultural University

(a) Agricultural universities should diversify their education programmes.

(b) Agricultural universities should set up centres/institutes for rural development.

National Council of Higher Education. Establishment of National Council of Higher Education was envisaged by the Programme of Action under NPE-1986. Functions of National Council of Higher Education are : advice to Government on policy, coordination of activities of various bodies in different fields, encouragement of interdicipline, and promotion of interfaces amongst different areas, allocation of resources, establishment and mechanism of common infrastructure and coordination of policy concerning external academic relations.

Review Committee suggested a two-tier structure of National Council of Higher Education.

(1) A Council of Ministers of Higher Education, the Ministers being those holding portfolios relating to education, agriculture, health, law and science and technology. It will be presided by Prime Minister. One of the Ministers may be Vice-chairman on rotation basis.

(2) A Council of Secretaries dealing with these subjects and Heads of the concerned institutions apart from Finance Secretary to Government of India and Secretary Planning Commission.

The policies will be formulated by this council and submitted to Council of Ministers for approval.

Technical and Management Education

Thrust Area Schemes. National level expert Committee should evaluate thrust area schemes. Expert Committee should take into consideration the following points :

(a) Proper utilisation of funds

(b) Achievement of the objectives of projects

(c) Adequate investment in projects

(d) Rearrangement of priorities

(e) Strengthening of monitoring system.

Community Polytechnics. The report of Kalbag Committee regarding financial requirements for community polytechnics and village centres should be reviewed and reviewed recommendations should be implemented in the first year of Eighth Five Year Plan.

AICTE. Regional offices of AICTE should be headed by senior functionaries. Regional offices should be given adequate devolution of authority and functions.

HT. Report of HT Review Committee should be carefully considered and decisions should be taken urgently.

Future Perspectives and Measures. Review Committee suggested specific actions related to the following aspects. Details of actions on these aspects are not described here.

(a) Improvement of quality and standards at all levels.

(b) Upgrading of infrastructure.

(c) Establishment of effective linkages with industry, national laboratories, development sectors and other institutions/ bodies.

(d) Assessment of manpower needs.

(e) Measures to prevent brain drain.

(f) Promotion of research and development.

(g) Steps to ensure cost-effectiveness.

(h) Special programmes for SC/ST, women and the physically handicapped.

(i) Entrepreneurship development.

(j) Continuing education and re-training programmes.

Resources for Education

1. Strategics for Raising Resources

   (a) Provide at least 6% of GNP for education.

   (b) All technical and professional education should be made self-financing. Education is viewed as involving the use of resources (inputs) that should be necessarily paid for by the beneficiaries as it confers on them greater employability (output).

2. Increase in Fees

   (a) There should be appropriate increase in fees payable by students going in for higher education.

   (b) Funds besides fee should in increased.

3. **Institutional Loans.** Strategy of institutional loans should be adopted. This will reduce pressure on Government resources.

4. **Financing Education by Nationalised Banks and Financial Institutions.** Nationalised Banks and Financial Institutions (IDBI, IFCI, ICICI, LIC) should finance/advance loans for higher education.

5. **Scholarships.** Provision of scholarship should be there for economically weaker sections of society.

6. Other Means of Raising Resources

   (a) Grant from the Government should be on matching basis. Community should collect contribution from community members and Government should contribute equal amount.

   (b) Scheme of foster parents to pay for elementary education of needy girls from weaker sections.

   (c) Collecton of educational cess.

   (d) Renting the facilities like conference hall, auditorium etc.

   (e) Constancy services by institutions.

   (f) Broad basing distance education.

   (g) Shift system in schools.

QUESTIONS

1. Write briefly the recommendations of Review Committee on NPE-1986 with specific reference to equity, social justice and education.
2. Discuss universalisation of elementary education in the context of Review Committee on NPW-1986.
3. Comment upon the following with specific reference to Review Committee on NPW-1986.

   (a) Adult and continuing education

   (b) Education and right to work

   (c) Higher education

   (d) Technical education and management

   (e) Resources for education.
4. List various guiding principles followed by Review Committee on NPW-1986.
5. Discuss views of Review Committee on NPW-1986 on early childhood care and education.

10

Medium of Teaching

In modern Indian education medium of instruction at schools, colleges and Universities is one of the current issues. There are about 380 languages or dialects of languages spoken in India. All these languages or dialects have been categorised under 14 languages in the Eighth Schedule of the Constitution. English was the medium of instruction before insdependence. The medium of instruction after independence was not English alone but mother tongue or regional languages have recieved special emphasis as medium of instruction and subjects of study.

Various Recommendations

Secondary Education Commission (1952-53). The mother tongue or the regional language should generally be the medium of instruction throughout school stage subject to the provision that for linguistic minorities, special facilities should be made available.

Kothari Commission (1964-66). Mother-tongue should be the medium of instruction at various levels of education (primary, secondary and tertiary).

The Committee of M.Ps on Education. It was recommended by the Committe of Members of Parliament on Education that Indian languages should be the media of instruction at all stages of education. This will help in the development of national integration or unity. Moreover, the development of Indian language should be one of the aims of education in India. If the media of instruction will not be modern Indian language, the creative energies of students can not be released and standard of education can not improve. Besides this, knowledge will not spread to masses and there will be a gulf or gap between intelligents and the masses.

This gap may widen also with the passage of time. The change in the medium of instruction should be within five years of span. The cooperation of academic community should be sought in this direction and the required resources of required nature should be provided.

National Policy of Education (1968). Govt Decisions

Govt of India took the following decisions on the language problem and problem of medium of instruction :

1. It will be obligatory for all the states to introduce the three language formula in their educational curriculum, extend it to the university stage and apply it strictly.
2. The UPSC Examination will be conducted in English, Hindi, and other national languages mentioned in the 8th schedule of Indian Constitution. All steps will be taken to implement this.
3. In the UPSC examinations, there will be compulsory papers in Hindi and English and in the case of candidates whose medium for UPSC examinations is Hindi, a paper in any other language mentioned in the schedule.

Languages in India according to the Eighth Schedule

Language	*Dialects*	*Language*	*Dialects*
1. Assamese	2	8. Marathi	65
2. Bengali	15	9. Oriya	24
3. Gujarati	27	10. Punjabi	29
4. Hindi	97	11. Sanskrit	3
5.Kannada	32	12. Tamil	22
6. Kashmiri	5	13. Telugu	36
7. Malayalam	14	14. Urdu	9
		Total	380

Now Nepali and Konkani and Manipuri languages have also been included in Eighth Schedule sindhi is also af them

4. To achieve the aforesaid purposes:

   (a) The State language of each state will become the medium of administration as well as instruction at the unversity stage as early as possible.

   (b) The standard of teaching of Hindi will have to be raised progressively in the schools as well as the university stage and

   (c) English will continue to be taught as language which has important role.

5. A phased programme for the development of Hindi and its progressive use will be prepared and carried out so that it can serve effectively as the official language of the union and the link language for the country. It will be ensured that the lines on which Hindi develops, conforms to the requirements of Article 851 of the Constitution.

6. A programme for the deveopment of national lanugages will also be prepared and implemented

Veiws of National Leaders. National leaders in India *e g* Mahatma Gandhi, Rabinder Nath Tagore always favoured the use of mother tongue as a medium of instruction. They opposed English as a medium of instruction in India.

Views of Sachar, (Punjab). Shri Bhim Sen Sachar, ex-chief Minister of Punjab during his period of Chief Ministership announced that parents are free to opt for Hindi or Punjabi as the medium of instruction for their wards. The state was divided into Hindi zone and Punjabi zone.

Present Scenario. The social demands vary from state to state. Presently, Boards of Education in different states are following English as well as their state languages as medium of instruction. NCERT is also publishing books in English as well as other Indian languages or even in tribal dialects. Certain institutions are working in this direction i.e. publication of books in various Indian languages.

Some efforts in this direction are highlighted below. These efforts are no doubt for development of specific languages but these development support education regional languages rather than English:

— Efforts for development of modern Indian languages

— Planning Commission has proposed to set up National Council for Promotion of Kashmiri Language during 2000-01 .

— Central Institute of Indian Languages, Mysore is making efforts through resarch studies on language analysis, language pedagogy, language technology, and language use.

— The National Council for promotion of Urdu Language is functioning since April 1996 as an autonomous body for the promotion of Urdu language and also for Arabic and Persian language.

— National Council for promotion of Sindhi Language has been set up for promotion of Sindhi language.

— Encouragement and financial assistance is being given for publication like encyclopaedias, dictionaries and book of knowledge, etc.

— Seminars/conferences/workshops are being organsied.

QUESTIONS

1. Discuss development with specific reference to medium of instruction after independence.
2. Describe medium of isntruction in context of National Policy on Education-1986 and decisions of Government of India.
3. Comment upon the following in context of medium of instruction:
   (a) Secondary Education Commission (1952-53).
   (b) Kothari Commission (1964-66)
   (c) Committee of M.Ps on Education.
   (d) National Policy on Education-1986.
4. Discuss the present status of medium of instruction at all the levels of education in India.

11

Elementary Education Universallsed

In emerging Indian society, there are a number of educational problems in the emerging Indian society. Universalisation of elementary education is one of the most important concerns today and in the near future. Significant developments have taken place to achieve the target since independence. We have moved forward but still the targets are to be achieved. India is a large country. We still have many problems to be handled with care with specific reference to the problem of universalisation of elementary education. The present chapter briefly highlights the efforts made in India before independence and after independance. The strategies adopted for universalisation have also been described. Lastly, the problems of wastage and stagnation have been discussed.

Historical Developments

Before Independence

1. Captain Wingate, the erstwhile Revenue Survey Commissioner in Bombay proposed to introduce compulsory education after collecting a cess during 1852.

2. The Government of Bombay appointed a Committee in 1906 to examine the feasibility of enforcing universal primary education but the Committee rejected the proposal.

3. Maharaja of Baroda introduced compulsory primary education in a part of his state.

4. Gopal Krishan Gokhale, member of Imperial Legislative Council introduced the first draft of law for compulsory education for the age group 6-10. He pleaded that unversal, free and compulsory education was essential for the development of the country. The bill was defeated but it developed awareness about education among masses. The First Act of compulsory education was passed in Bombay in 1918. It is known as Patel' s Act as it was moved by Vithalbhai Patel. It was mainly for children in the age group 6-11 in the rural Bengal, Bihar, Orissa, Punjab, U.P., Madras etc.

5. Mahatma Gandhi moved the Resolution on Basic Education at Wardha Congress Conference in 1937 and appealed that a national policy be adopted for free and compulsory education for all children in the age group 6-14.

After Independence

1. Article 45 Article 45 of Indian Constitution states "The State shall endeavour to provide within a period ten years from the commencement of constitution, for free compulsory education for all children until they complete the age of fourteen years."

2. Kothari Commission (1964-66). Government of India appointed Education Commission in 1964 popularly known as Kothari Commission (1964-66) to advise the Government on the national pattern of education and suggest measures to accomplish the goals of universal education at the earliest possibie. The commission pointed out the role of education in National Development.

The Kothari Commission devised the following strategy for fulfilling the Constitutional Directive:

1. Each State and even each District would prepare a perspective plan for the development of primary education taking into consideration the stage of development already reached and local condition and problems.

2. Each State and District should go ahead at the best pace it can.

3. All the areas in the countries should be able to provide five years of good and effective education to all the children by 1975-76 and seven years of such education by 1985-86.
4. The commission was hopeful that enrolment shall increase from 50 million in 1965-66 to 125 million in 1985-86 and enrolment at the lower primary stage in Classes I-V was expected to rise from 37 million in 1965-66 to 72 million in 1975-76 and 76 milion in 1985-86. The Commission was hopeful that the enrolment in Classes V-VIII shall increase from 13 million in 1965-66 to 32 million in 1975-76 and 49 million in 1985-86.
5. The Commission laid emphasis on the reduction of wastage and stagnation and ensured that every child who enters Class I would progress regularly from year to year and reach Class V and not less than 80% would reach Class VII.
6. The Commission also emphasized for qualitative improvement and programme of parental education
7. The impact of recommedation of The Kothari Commission was that there was a rapid expansion at the lower primary stage.
8. National Education Policy: 1979. National Education Policy, 1979 emphasized on the free and compulsory education and suggested that education up to the elemenatry level should be general and not specialised and should give pupils a confident command of language and two subjects and a scientific attitude. Elementary education should develop the personality and character of students. The Government should formulate a scheme for non-formal education for drop-outs. It also pointed out that there is no need to change approach to learning process at the primary classes. Contents should be restructured keeping in view traditional values, composite culture of the country and present reality and vision of the cummon future.
9. Early Childhood Care and Education (ECCE): Keeping in view the poor national targets of universal education after independence, a network of ECCE facilities should be established in all the tribal blocks, slums, and scheduled caste population areas.

10. National Policy on Education 1986: The National Policy on Education 1986 shifted emphasis from enrolment to retention and completion by all children of at least five years of education. Efforts were expected to be made to ensure the provision of certain minimum essential facilities in every primary school in the country.

    National Policy on elementary education was guided in free India on the following two considerations:

    1. Educational facilities must be expanded rapidly so as to provide universal education as early as possible.
    2. The qualitative improvement i.e. improvement of teachers, syllabi, teaching methods, textbooks, building, equipment etc.

    New Policy has put emphasis on the removal of disparities and to equalise educational opportunity by attending to the specific needs of those who have been denied equality. Disparities are between men and women, scheduled castes and non-scheduled castes, scheduled tribes and non-scheduled tribes, rural and urban areas, advanced and backward states and between various regions in a state. Disparities have increased and quality of education has also gone down in proportion taits quantity.

11. Central Advisory Board of Education Committee 1991 (CBSE-1991): The CBSE Committee was constituted in July 1991 to review the implementation of National Policy on Education-1986. A Report was submitted in 1992 and the reformulation of National Policy on education was recommended. It was mentioned that it was not possible to increase the number and spread of institutions as well as enrolment. The Board was of the view that universalisation of elementary education in its totality was still an illusive goal and much ground was yet to be covered in this regard. The drop-out rate was found significant. Retention was low. Wastage was considerable. Participation of girls in upper primary classes was low. The Board suggested participative planning. Teachers and villagers were required to formulate family-wise and child-wise design of action to ensure that every child regularly attended school and completed at least five years of schooling and activity based process of learning.

12. Role of Judiciary in India: The response of judiciary to the right of education has always been positive in particular to the children of weaker sections of the society. Judiciary has shown courage to direct Government to provide better and adequate educational facilities, economic support and proper atmosphere to children belonging to lower strata of society at least up to primary level. According to Directive Principles of State Policy, children up to 14 years of age are supposed to be in school. Judiciary observes that the Directive is implemented. Social justice is also an area where Judiciary have played a significant role. The Supreme Court has taken stand for free and complusory education under Article 45.

Strategies for Universalisation of Primary Education

Strategies adopted for universalisation of primary education in India are briefly discussed below :

Strategy of Universal Enrolment: The programme of universal elementary education aims at bringing every child into school and to see that he or she remains at school till he or she completes the elementary education on age 14. Previously we emphasized on enrolment drives only. As a result of this, enrolment was found more but only a few continued to acquire an effective literacy. Another problem observed was that students in each class were of different ages. *i.e.* every class was heterogenous.

The Working Group on Universalisation of Elementary Education in its Interim Report (1978) recommended formal as well as non-formal education. According to the Report, every child shall continue to learn in the age group 6-14 on a full-time basis if possible, and on a part-time basis, if necessary.

Ishwar Bhai Patel Committee (1977) (also known as Review Committee on Curriculum for 10 year school) recommended for reduction of formal instruction to minimum of 2'/2 to 3 hours for children in Classes I-IV/V. But it was felt that as first step, the instructional hours in Classes I-III should be reduced to 3 hours a day.

Programme of Action mentions that 22 percent of the enrolled are outside 6-11 age group and hence are mostly over age. Emphasis has been given on non-formal and formal education. Emphasis has also shifted from enrolment to retention and completion by all children of at least 5 years of education. Enrolment drives would be replaced by systematic house to house survey in which the teachers in cooperation with the village community would discuss with the parents the importance of schooling and regularity of attendance. Children unable to participate in whole-day schools should attend non-formal education centres. It should be ensured that every child in every family receives instruction. All children should, therefore, regularly attend school or non-formal education centres.

Strategy of Universal Retention. Elementary education should be child-centred by making it joyful, inventive and satisfying learning activity rather than a system of role, cheerless and authoritarian instruction. Curricular and co-curricular activities should be made interesting and meaningful. Corporal punishment should be banned by all means. Non-retention Policy would be effectively implemented upto Class VIII. A comprehensive system of incentives and support services should be provided for all girls and children of economically weaker sections of the community.

Following points are related to the strategy of universal retention:

1. Establishment of day care centres for pre-school children and infants-as a pan of strengthening of ICDS, provision of adequate support of the ongoing programme and by establishment of network of new centres.

2. Provision to the girls of all families below the poverty line two sets of free uniforms, free textbooks and stationery and attendance incentives.

3 Free transportation in State Roadways buses to children attending elementary schools.

4. A comprehensive programme of rewards and recognition will be created for individuals and institutions who contribute in a significant manner to the retention of students in primary schools or non-formal centres.

5. The Operation Blackboard has been proposed to ensure provision of minimum essential facilities in primary school—material facilities as well as learning equipment. The term "operation" implies that there is an urgency in

this programme, that goals are clear and well-defined and that Government and the people are determined to achieve these goals within a pre-determined time frame. Operation Blackboard envisages: (1) two reasonably large rooms that are usable in all weather; (2) necessary toys and games materials ; (3) blackboard; (4) maps; (5) charts and (6) other learning materials.

6. One more teacher should be appointed in single teacher schools. One of two teachers should be a woman. Male teachers serving in remote areas should be given special training. These efforts will lead to qualitative improvement.

Strategy of Universal Provision of Facilities: Universal provision of facilities for primary classes (Classes I-V) and middle school classes is considered the first step towards universalisation of primary education. According to Programme of Action (1986), "All the State Governments will ensure that all habitations with a population of 300 (200 in cases of tribal, hilly and desert areas) will be provided a primary school within the Seventh Plan. Effort will also be made on the lines of Mobile Creches to set up special school for specific duration for building and construction workers and other categories of people who shift their residence."

The Working Group on Universalisation of Elementary Education in its Interim Report observed that in opening new schools, general policy adopted is to open them first in bigger villages without schools and gradually take up the smaller villages. Priority should be given for opening schools for tribal areas. Ashram schools should be there for tribal childrci

The Programme of Action (1986) also recommended for preparing a Master Plan of Universal Provision of Facilities for Elementary Education.

Wastage and Stagnation

Removal of Disparities. Necessary steps are recommended to remove disparities among individuals, castes, areas and so on. This is extremely essential for universal recognition of elementary education. A few examples are as follows:

1. A number of scholarships should be introduced.
2. Free reading and writing materials are to be supplied.

3. Uniforms are to be provided freely.
4. Mid-day meals is to be given to the children of weaker section.

Development of New Curriculum. Curriculum is one of the major factors which is responsible for the wastage and stagnation and hence is a major aspect to be looked into the issue of universalisation of primary education. Curriculum should be related to the life needs and aspirations of the people. It should be dynamic as well as flexible suiting to the children with diverse cultural, social and economic background. Co-curricular activities should be organised and work education should be given due place in school curriculum. According to Ishwar Bhai Patel Committee (1977), there is a need for more creative and joyful activities than formal instruction.

Teaching Methods and Teaching Aids: Methods of teaching should be according to the needs of the students. Play-way methods should be followed at the primary level. The teaching aids should be simple, relevant and interesting. Special methods and learning materials should be developed for tribal and rural areas. Above steps on methods and teaching aids will help in the universalisation of primary education.

Improving Teacher Education Programmes and Supervision: Teachers are not properly trained in dealing with students. They need proper training in the use of curriculum according to students' needs. The teacher education programme should be improved so that desired training may be imparted both in service and as well as pre-service. The effective teacher education programmes will help in universalisation of primary education.

Parent Education: Lack of awareness about education among parents is a major problem in achieving the target of universalisation of education. Parents who do not realize the significance of education in our lives need to be educated through the use of mass media and other well planned activities. Parent-Teacher-Associations (PTA) are useful in involving parents of enrolled children. Radio, television, films, slides, newspapers, journals, books and other activities can contribute effectively in developing awareness among masses the significance of education in personal, social and national development programme.

Non-Formal Education Programmes: Universalisation of Primary education cannot be achieved only through formal means of education. Part-time education for non-enrolled children and drop-outs in the age group 6-14 is a must to achieve the target. According to New Policy on Education (1986), highest priority should be given to solving the problem of drop-outs. Micro-planning should be there for this purpose. Retention of students should be ensured. According to Programme of Action (1986), modern technological tools (such as solar packs for provision of power in non-formal education centres, audio-visual aids, radio-cassette player) are useful in non-formal education.

QUESTIONS

1. Describe the efforts made towards the universalisation of elementary education before independence and after independance.
2. Describe efforts made after independence to solve the problem of universalisation of elementary education.
3. Describe the strategies adopted in India to solve the problem of Universalisation of elementary education.
4. What are the factors that are acting as constraints with specific reference to universalisation of elementary education in India.
5. Describe the steps that should be taken to deal with the problem of wastage and stagnation with specific reference to universalisation of elementary education in India.

12

Education for Women

In a country, its economy depends upon education of the masses. Women and men both are to be treated equally in case we want the development of the nation. The social problems are in our way. People do not attach importance to the education of girls. Emerging Indian society demands challenging roles on the part of women. The efforts have been made since independence on the education of girls/women. University Education Commission, Secondary Education Commission, Indian Education Commission, National Policy on Education and Review Committee of National Policy on Education have emphasized on the education of women. The present chapter deals briefly the recent efforts in dealing with the problem of women education in India. The Historical view can be referred back to earlier chapters.

National Policy on Education on Empowerment of Women in Modern India

The views of National Policy on Empowerment of women are briefly discussed here under the following headings :

1. Education for Equality and social justice
2. Education for women's equality
3. Targets under National Policy on Education 1986.

Education for Equality and Social Justice. Empowerment of women through education was emphasized in the National Policy on Education-1986. New Policy on-Education-1986 emphasizes on the removal of disparities and equalisation of educational opportunities by attending to the special needs of those who have been denied equality so far. Education for equality according to NPE-1986 covers the following :

(a) Education for women's equality

(b) The education of scheduled castes

(c) The education of scheduled tribes

(d) Other educationally backward section and areas

(e) Minorities

(f) The handicapped.

(g) Adult education

Education for Women's Equality. We are concerned here with education for women's equality. The empowerment of women through education was emphasized under the major heading *i. e.*, education for women's equality. Following facts are mentioned in this context.

(a) Education will be used as an agent of basic change in the status of women. In order to neutralise the accumulated distortions of the past, there will be a well-conceived edge in favour of women. The national education system will play a positive, interventionist role in the empowerment of women. It will foster the development of new values through redesigned decision-makers and administrators and the active involvement of educational institution. This will be an act of faith and social engineering. Women studies will be promoted as a part of various courses and educational institutions encouraged to take up active programmes to farther women's development.

(b) The removal of women's illiteracy and obstacles inhibiting their access to and retention in elementary education will receive overriding priority through provision of special support services, setting of time targets, and effective monitoring. Major emphasis will be laid on women's participation in vocational, technical and professional education at different levels. The policy of non-discrimination will be pursued vigorously to eliminate sex stereotyping in non-traditional occupation, as well as in existing and emergent technologies.

Programme of Action 1986 : Targets

1. A phased time-bound programme of elementary education for girls particularly up to the primary stage by 1990.

2. A phased time-bound programme of adult education for women in the age group 15-35 by 1995.
3. Increased women access to vocational, technical, professional education and to existing and emergent technologies and
4. Review and reorganisation of the educational activities to ensure that it makes a substantial contribution towards women's equality and creation of appropriate cells or units.

Problems of Women Education and their Remedies

Committee on the Status of Women in India, National Plan of Action for Women, National Policy on Education-1986 and National Perspective Plan-1990 studied and analysed that there is poor progress in girl's education/ women education. Studies reveal that women of modern India are playing role in different fields which were earlier monopolised by men. For instance, politics, science and technology, journalism, administration etc. In certain areas, women have proved better than men e.g. medicine, teaching, nursing, social work etc.

Problems. The progress in the education of women in modren India is slow. The major problems related to women education in India are briefly described below :

(1) Domestic Duty:

(a) Girls are required to devote time in domestic works at a very young age.

(b) In poor section of society, girls even perform such duties as-bringing potable water, taking food to fields for parents engaged in work and looking after their young siblings.

(c) Girls in poor sections of society are required to work as paid and unpaid workers.

(d) Parents do not understand the importance of education of daughters. They give preference to boys as compared to girls.

(2) Social Problems: Marriage of girls especially early marriage is one of the important factors/problems of women/girls education. It is serious problem in certains States in India, e.g. U.P, M.P., Bihar, Rajasthan and Gujarat.

(3) Inadequate Facilities: There are many villages where there are no schools. In case the schools are there they lack physical facilities. According to an estimate 44 per cent of the primary schools do not have pucca building. Fifty nine per cent schools do not have drinking water supply.

(4) Sex Bias in Curricula and Policies: The curricula cover topics which show role of women as home makers, wives and mother. Women should be held in curricula in modern roles. Contents in books sometime pose women as non-achievers, timid and dependent. Sex bias in curricula should be removed. Policies should be there which may encourage women education.

Remedies

Use of Media for Promoting Awareness Among Masses for Women Education/Girls Education. Media can play a significant role in developing awareness among masses regarding the education of women/girls. This solution to girl/women education was also emphasized in the National Policy on Education-1986 and National Perspective Plan for Women (1988-2000 AD).

Teachers, social workers, personnel concerned with education, NGO's (non-governmental organisations) can play significant role in promoting awarencess among masses regarding the importance of women education under the present conditions of Indian society.

Assistance in the Form of Cash or Kind for Primary Education. Following steps can be useful for promoting girls/ women education :

1. Some compensatory economic assistance should be given to parents for sparing their girl children for education.
2. Social service agencies or Government may extend assistance in the shape of cash and kind to the girls of poor families. There is a scheme in Maharashtra known as Savitribai Phule Foster Parent Scheme'. Under this scheme, poor families are economically helped for the completion of primary education of their daughters. Well to do parents and organisation adopt girl child and help in completing primary education. Uniform, textbooks, stationery and food materials are supplied.

3. There is a scheme in Tamil Nadu known as "Foster Parent-Scheme". This scheme was launched to celebrate the SAARC Years for the Girl Child Social service minded people adopt girls reading in Class 1 to Class VIII and they assist parents by paying Rs. 250/- per year to the parents of the girl child for her education.

Employment for Educated Women: Educated women should be provided opportunities of employment in various sections of the society.

No Sex Bias in Curricula: Contents covered in textbooks should not deal with reading material which shows sex bias. The curricula should be revised accordingly.

Provision of Adequate Physical Facilities: According to National Policy on Education-1986, scheme of Operation Blackboard was launched during 1987-1988. Under this scheme every primary school should have at least two all weather rooms, a second teacher preferably a female teacher in single teacher schools and essential teaching and learning materials.

Improvement in Quality of Teachers and School: Environment Quality of teachers should be improved. Their qualification and competencies should be better. The teaching-learning enviornment should be good so that students may like to attend school and develop interest in studies.

Recommendations of Various Commissions or Commitees

Please refer to the following for the recommendations of various Committees/Commissions on women education :

1. University Education Commission (1948-49)
2. Secondary Education Commission (1952-53)
3. Indian Education Commission (1964-66)
4. NPE-1986
5. Review Committee 1992

QUESTIONS

1. Comment upon empowerment of women in the light of National Policy on Education 1986.
2. Discuss remedial measures to deal with the factors or constraints with specific reference to education of women in emerging Indian society.
3. Comment upon the following :

   (a) Problems of women education

   (b) Remedial steps for the education of women in India.

13

Education for the Weak

The international goal of education is 'Education for All'. We today realise that standard of living can be improved through specific efforts. Education is one of the factors that contributes to capital formation, an important element for economic development. We can not ignore weaker sections, i.e. scheduled castes, scheduled tribes, women, backward classes (including other back ward classes) handicapped, etc. The weaker sections includes all individuals who are weaker with specific reference to economy, politics, physical development, social development, emotional development, intellectual (cognitive) development etc. The present chapter highlights efforts made by India in the education of masses with specific reference to weaker sections in India.

Meaning of Weaker Sections

To quote Indian constitution :

"We, the people of India, having solemly resolved to constitute India into a sovereign, democratic and socialist republic and to secure to all its citizens Justice (social, economic and political), liberty of thought, expression, belief and worship and equality of status and opportunity and to promote among them all fraternity assuring the dignity of the individual and unity of the Nation."

The analysis of the above constitutional provision, point out the following goals:

1. Development of India into a sovereign, democratic and socialist republic.

2. Provision of economic, social and political justice to Indian citizens.

3. Provision of liberty of thought, expression, belief and worship.
4. Provision of equality of status.
5. Provision of equality of opportunities.
6. Promotion of fraternity.
7. Maintenance of integrity of Indian citizens.
8. Development of national unity i.e. emotional and national integration.

Meaning of Weaker Section of Society

Equality of opportunities in eveiv sphere of life : economic, social, cultural, educational, political, spiritual, religious, etc. Reservations in opportunities is for maintenance of equity So, the concepts of equity and equality are for all such individuals who on certain parameters, are below as compared to others who are termed as normals or advanced. These individuals may be called as weaker sections or deprived or disadvantaged sections of the society.

Concept of Equality of Educational Opportunities

Equality in education means equal availability of educational opportunities for every qualified person irrespective of sex, caste, religion, language, race, colour, political opinion, nation or social origin, economic condition or birth. Equality does not assume that all individuals are basically equal in capacities. Each individual should get opportunities as warranted by his innate capacities. No one should be stopped fromgoing up except when he himself lacks the ability to go up. Views of certain authorities are briefly described below :

V.R. Taneja. The equality of educational opportunity implies the provision of:

(1) free education upto a given level which constitutes the principal entry point to the national, labour force. Thus eliminating the economic source of inequality of opportunities;

(2) differential educational opportunities suiting the needs, abilities and aspirations of student; and

(3) state help in the form of scholarships, subsidies and loans in case a student is not able to maintain himself.

B.R.Goyal. *B.R. Goyal* (1983) presents the following views on the concept of equality of educational opportunities with specific reference of India :

(1) Every Indian should get a minimum level of education.

(2) In the distribution of educational opportunities, the innate ability and aptitude of the students should be the main criterion.

(3) Instead of a common school system, we should have a neighbourhood school system in India, and instead of common curriculum we should have a need based curriculum which may develop competencies in the learners.

(4) In case, a student is not able to maintain himself, he should be helped to avail educational opportunities by means of scholarship or even loans.

(5) Availing of educational opportunities should go, hand in hand with the recognition of educational merit as a means of securing job or a position in life.

General View. The general view on the concept of equality of educational opportunity is that it constitutes the following three dimensions:

(1) Equality of access to education.

(2) Equality in utility of education (common school system).

(3) Equality of social status derived from educational attainments.

Concept of Equity

Equity means fairness or impartiality in the availability of opportunities to every individual of the society. In the light of social fairness, it is fair to follow the policy of reservations for scheduled castes, scheduled tribes, backward classes, women, people from rural area, sportsmen, freedom fighter, ex-military persons and their wards, etc. Constitutional amendments have been made from time to time in this context in India.

Concept of Equality and Equity in Education

Meaning. Equality and equity means equal and fair availability of educational opportunities to every individual after elimination of all factors which create inequity and exploitation.

Equality and Equity in Education at Various Levels

Primary Level. The State has the responsibility to provide free and compulsory education, for all children until they complete the age of fourteen years. It means that there should be universal enrolment, universal provision of physical facilities and universal retention. The universal enrolment, provision of infrastructure and retention is called as universalisation of primary education. The curriculum should be based upon basic needs of individuals or there should be basic education.

Secondary Level. The equality and equity in education at secondary level is the availability of educational opportunities for individual on the basis of their diversified interests, aptitudes and capacities. Individual differences in all aspects (physical, intellectual, social and emotional) are observed at this stage. Another important aspect of equality at this level is the availability of vocational and technical education opportunities besides general education. The population at the secondary level is considered active from production point of view.

Higher Level or Tertiary Level. The meaning of equality at higher level is the availability of educational opportunities on the basis of merit. There are reservation of seats from the point of view of social equity.

Need and Importance of Equality and Equity in Education

Development of Egalitarian Society. Egalitarian social system means social system that favours the doctrine of equal rights, benefits and opportunities for all citizens. This type of social system is the aim of Indian democracy. Education is one of the instruments which can bring a social change of this type.

Upward Social Mobility Within and Outside the Framework of Caste. Caste system is one of the major problems in bringing about a desirable change in Indian society today. In the earlier times, caste, sex and religion were linked with education. Profession was caste based. There was hardly any relationship between equality and educational opportunity for the masses in general. New educational opportunities during the middle of 20th century affected the social structure and function. There was a gradual dissociation of occupation from caste. Sanskritisation and Westernisation are the factors for upward social mobility of people in the middle of 20th century.

Sanskritisation is the process where caste groups or sections of these being benefitted by the new education and employment opportunities, try to use high in the caste heirarchy by claiming a higher status. Westernisation is the process where individuals get education in the Public School and Convents and follow modern occupations which are more remunerative and adopt a Westernized style of life. The Western system of education is responsible for spreading egalitarian idea and scientific rationality. These ideas became the guiding spirit in the fight for equality of opportunities during the middle 20th century in India. For example, the Government of India has taken positive steps for the upliftment of the weaker sections of society to make the system of social stratification more egalitarian. Equality of opportunities in respect of education gained significance. This is helping us in removing the evils of caste system, promoting upwards social mobility both within and inside the framework of caste. Today thrust is being placed on the equality of educational opportunities to achieve a more egalitarian system of social stratification, where there is an open chance for an individual to achieve a higher social status.

Elimination of Factors of Discrimination in Education

On December 10, 1948, the idea of equality was highlighted in the Universal Declaration of Human Rights by the General Assembly of the United Nations where, *inter-alia* the principle of "non-discrimination." and "right to education" were strongly advocated. These two principles inherited the concept of equality of opportunity in education which was elaborated on December 14,1960 by the General conference of UNESCO (Taneja, 1983). Factors of discrimination which are obstacles in social change are: sex, colour, race, language, caste, religion, political opinion, national or social origin, economic condition, birth etc. All these factors have no place in the concept of equality and equity in education. Equality and equity in education is needed to form human capital which is one of the major factors in economic and national development of all countries of the world. In case, we go on using factors of discrimination, the human resources and consequently economy will not develop.

Efforts for Education of Weaker Sections

School Education : Primary and Secondary

(1) *Common School System.* Indian Education Commission (1964-66) recommended the common school system in India keeping in weaker sections of the society.

(2) *Neighbourhood Schools* The idea of common school system was further modified and the concept of neighbourhood school developed (Goyal, 1983). Curriculum of neighbourhood school system is based upon the basic needs and it should develop skills and competencies to cope with problematic situations in day-to-day life.

(3) *Navodaya Vidyalayas.* Navodaya Vidyalayas were opened for imparting quality education to childen. .

(4) *Reservation of Seat in Public Schools.* Policy of reservations of seats has been followed for public schools to enforce equity in education.

(5) *Unfversalisation of Primary Education.* Universal provision of education has been made at the primary level for the population of children of age group 5-14.

(6) *Formal and Non-formal Programmes for secondary Education.* Formal and non-formal (correspondence courses) are there for secondary level. Vocationalisation has been introduced as this population of students is considered productive in nature. Individuals of age group 15-65 are considered to get involved in programmes of production and economic development.

Higher Education. The education opportunities at the higher level are provided on the basis of merit. Reservation policy is also followed at this stage to provide equity in education besides equality.

Provision Under the National Policy on Education 1986. The National Policy on Education—1986 has emphasized on the removal of disparities and thus making the concept of equality in education more impartial or fair keeping in view overall desirable social change leading to economic development of the countiy. A brief description of these provisions is given below:

Women Education. Women education is one of major problems of Indian society. There is a lack of awareness among people about women education. Now it is being realised in general that women can contribute to national and economic development. The Government of India has also emphasized in the New Policy on Education that special emphasis be given to women education. States are taking necessary steps to encourage women to participate and avail the available educational opportunities in India and thereby, then enabling them contribute to the self and national development programmes.

Education of Scheduled Castes. Following steps are being taken to provide equity to scheduled caste students. Enrolment drives are being initiated to enroll students of age group 5-14 years. Scholarship schemes are being adopted for scheduled caste students from first class to 10th class in order to improve their prospects of receiving essential education. Teachers from scheduled castes are being recruited. The location of schools, Balwadis and Adult Educational Centres are being decided in such a way which may facilitate maximum participation of the children belonging to scheduled castes. Research is being conducted to search new method which may motivate them for education of their children.

Education of Scheduled Tribes. Following steps arc being undertaken to provide equity to children of scheduled tribes:

* Priority is being given for opening schools in tribal areas.
* The language of tribal people is being used in the beginning.
* The training in teaching is being given to tribal youth with the aim that they may serve their own localities through teaching.
* Priority is being given to open "Anganwadis" and the Adult Education Centres in tribal areas.
* Steps are being taken to enroll children belonging to scheduled tribes.

Education of Educationally Backward Sections of Areas. The attention is being paid more to the education of minority groups without any social injustice. The; are free to establish and administer their own educational institutions for furthering the cause of education and protection of their language and culture.

Education of Handicapped. Special attention is being given to the education of handicapped with the aim to integrate physically and mentally handicapped children with the general community as equal partners in order to prepare them to cope with day-to-day life problems like normal individuals. The following steps are being undertaken to achieve the above mentioned central aim:

(1) The children having minor handicaps are being encouraged to study with normal children with an objective to develop confidence in them to lead the life like normal children.

(2) There is a provision of hostels at district level for handicapped children.

(3) The facilities for vocatioal and technical education programmes to enable then to deal with the problems of handicapped children.

(4) Voluntary orgnaisations are being encouraged for making desirable efforts towards the education of handicapped.

Adult Education for Weaker Sections. Formal education is being given through formal institutions at all levels. But, illiterate propulation within the age group of 15-35 years may get education through non-formal means. The Government of India in the New Policy on Education—1986 has emphasized the education of adults. This policy highlights that the Centre and State Governments, the poilitical parties the mass media and educational institutions must contribute to mass literacy programmes. Teachers, students, youth, voluntary oganisations, employees, etc. should be motivated to participate in the adult education programmes.

Distance Education for Weaker Sections. Distance education facilities arc contributing significantly to providing equality and equity in education. Suppose, one is not in a position to get admission in any of the formal institutions for one reason or the other, he or she may draw the lenefits of education through distance education programmes. The Universities are providing this educational facility. Open Universities are there in India for this purpose at the state and national level. For example, the Indira

Gandhi National Open University was opened in 1985. The State and Central Universities have independent Departments of Distance Education.

Education of Scheduled Castes : Views of M.S. Swaminathan

M.S. Swaminathan (1982) then, member of Planning Commission. (NP), in the National Seminar on Educational Development of Scheduled Castes at the Indian Institute of Education, Pune, on 30th January, 1982 highlighted various educational aspects about scheduled castes. A brief reference is given below

1. Population of Scheduled Castes in India: Scheduled castes constitute 15% of the total population of India. The attention is required on their economic, educational and social development.
2. Efforts of British Government. No serious efforts were made by British Government before independence.
3. Efforts after Independence. Efforts were made by Indian Govt. for educational, social and economic development after independence.

To quote Article 45

"The State shall endeavour to provide within a period of ten years from the commencement of the Constitution for free and compulsory education for all children until they complete the age of 14 years.

Article 46

"The state shall promote with special care of the education and economic interests of the weaker sections of the people and particularly, of the scheduled castes and scheduled tribes and shall protect them from social injustice and all forms of exploitation."

Educational facilities here provided after Constitutional provisions. State Governments, Central Government and non-official organisations contributed to the education of this weaker sections of the society. More co-ordination among State, Centre and Non-official organisation is needed. Efforts were made in successive Five year Plans in the following areas:

1. Special schemes for pre and post-matric scholarships.
2. Educational incentives like provision of books, stationery, uniforms, coaching classes, boarding, grants, hostel facilities, etc.

Result of Efforts

* Increase in Scholarships: 105 lakhs SC students got scholarship benefits by 1985.
* Increase in Literacy Rate: Literacy rate a males was 2.4 (against Indian literacy rate of 39) and females was 6.4 (against Indian literacy rate of 19).
* Literacy rates increased both in case of males as well as females.
* Increase in enrolment.
* Coeffecient of equality improved in general courses and vocational courses.
* Wastage and stagnation was reduced.
* Retention in schools increased. Efforts required in the following areas:
* Training of Teachers.
* Sensitisation of teachers towards weaker sections during in-service teachers progarnmes.
* Teacher should come in contact with parents to make them realise about the significance of education.
* Teachers can provide educational and vocational guidance.
* Opening of non-formal/part-time classes for weaker sections of the society.
* Efforts for increasing literacy rate of scheduled castes is needed.
* Enrolment is to be increased.
* Understanding the educational handicaps of SCs. We should try to understand the socio-economic handicaps of scheduled castes.

* The following objectives as given in 5th Five Year Plan. The working Group on the Development of SCs should be kept in mind:

  — Number of SCs for education at different levels including adult education centres.
  — Identification of constraints of SCs.
  — Identification of programmes, financial requirements & other concerns for taking or consideration of SCs.
  — Planning
  — Time and action
  — Schedule preparation.
  — Implementation, evaluation & remedial measures.

Challenges for the Future

Making Arrangement for Opportunity Cost for Ensuring Cent-Per Cent Enrolment at the Primary stage. To ensure cent-per cent enrolment, we will have to take into account the opprotunity cost of education for families engaged in agriculture labour and the like, institution of appropriate scholarship (a sort of compensation for the opportunity cost).

Improvement in Performance through Specific Programmes. Organisation of preparatory training. Remedial teaching, Special coaching and Entrance coaching for improving standards of performance at each level.

Admissions. Admissions in various institutions in due proportions.

Provision / Facilities. Provisions like scholarship, fellowships, associateships and other incentives (free textbooks, free uniforms, mid-day meals)

Hostel Facilities. Hostel arrangements should be adequate.

Elimination of Wastage. Steps should be taken to eliminate the problem of wastage.

Reservation. Steps should be taken to ensure at least 15% representation of SCs in the teaching and non-teaching staff.

Needbased Human Resource Development. The steps should be taken to organise activities for needbased human resource development in SCs. This should result into the development of awareness and strengths for management of their own development.

Reduction in the Role of Agents. Steps to develop the awareness about deducation of the role of agents/ middlemen in their economic activities (selt-employment activities.)

Education of SC and ST : Indian Education Commission (1964-66)

"One of the important social objectives of education is to equalise opportunity enabling the backward or under priveleged classes and individuals to use education as a lever for improvement of their condition. Every-society that values social justice and is anxious to improve the lot of the common man and cultivate all available talent must ensure progressive equality of opportunity to all sections of the population. This is the only guarantee for the building up of an egalitarian and human society in which exploitation of the weak will be minimised."

Suggestions for Education of Scheduled Classes and Scheduled Tribes

Teacher Behaviour. Behaviour of the teacher towards the children of these sections of the society matters a lot. Sympathetic and encouraging behaviour may provide them support for going ahead towards the achievement of educational aims and objectives.

No Discrimination by Teaching Staff. The teaching staff should not discriminate with these children in any manner as far as the school atmosphere or environment is concerned.

Avoid Use of Words Highlighting their Caste. The caste should not be highlighted in any situation *e.g.* may be taking attendance in the class, morning assemble activities or routine working of the educational institution.

Equal Provision of Facilities for Participation in Curricular and Extra-Curricular Activities. The involvement of students belonging to these castes in varied types of curricular and co-curricular activities should be equally encouraged. There should be no element of thinking lower of them and discriminating them.

Parent-Teacher Relationship. The parents of the children should be contacted. Different programmes can be organised for this purpose. The over all purpose of these contact programmes should be to develop the sense of equality in all respects. They should be made aware of the importance of education for economic, social and cultural development. The cooperation of parents can be sought in the development of children.

Motivation of Parents for Joint Adult Education Centres. Teacher should encourage the parents of the children of weaker section to join adult education centres in their localities. This will develop awareness about role of education in one's life.

Special Teaching Programmes. Special leading activites like remedial teaching, special coaching for academically bright or poor students etc. can be organised. The financial resources can be explored may be from the Government funds or social organisations, commerical organisation, individuals etc.

Development of Hobbies and Participation in Sports, Cultural Programmes. Participation in all activities should be encouraged by head and teachers of the school.

9. Provision of Financial Assistances and Other Incentives. Various programmes for financial assitance, free instructional materials, free concessions, free uniform, free transport, even free accomodation etc. should be made.

Education of SC and ST : National Policy on Education (1986, 1992)

The National Policy on Education (NPE)—1986 as updated in 1992 (Review Committee) suggested measures regarding scheduled castes, scheduled tribes and educationally backward and minorities:

Relaxation in the norms for opening primary schools norms for opening of primary schools have been relaxed in case of ST habitations to have a primary school within one kilometer walking distance from habitations having a population of 200 persons instead of the general criteria of 300 persons.

No Tution Fee. Tuition fee for SC and ST students has been abolished in Government schools in all states upto upper primary level. Most of the States have abolished tution fees for students at senior secondary level. The students are provided incentives like free textbooks, uniforms, stationery, school bags etc.

Relaxation in Admission, Reservation of Seats

* The relaxations in admission criteria is given.
* Seats are reserved for admissions in various institutions *e.g.* schools, colleges, universities, IITs, medical colleges, engineering colleges, professional insitutions.

Progammes for Improving Academic Skills and Linguistic Proficiency. Training Programmes are organised for SC & ST students for developing competencies for various entrance tests *e.g.* IAS, professional colleges, services in general.

Scholarships

* National scholarships at the secondary level.
* Fellowship.
* Research associateship.
* UGC awards.
* Reduction in percentage in eligibility of National Eligibility Test (NET) for appointment as lecturers (from 55% to 50%) for SC & ST students.

Textbooks in Tribal Languages. The central institute of Indian Languages Mysore prepares textbooks, primers, grammar books , dictionaries, bilingual textbooks, etc. to facilitate translation from regional languages into tribal languages. The Institute has worked in 75 tribal and border languages. NCERT has published textbooks in tribal dialects and instructional materials in 15 tribal dialects.

Literacy Rate. Literacy rate among SC / ST women is less than 10%. Centre is giving more attention to districts where literacy rate is less.

Priroity of Specific Programmes in Areas of Concentration ofSC and ST. Priority is being given for specific programmes of Government listed below in areas of concentration of SC and ST.

(1) District Primary Education Programme (DPEP)

(2) Lok Jumbish

(3) Shiksha Karmi

(4) Non-formal education

(5) Mid-day meals or National Programme for Nutritional Support to Primary Education

DPEP. The District Primary Education Programme (DPEP) was launched in 1994 as a major initiative to achieve the objective of universalisation of primary education (UPE). The Programme takes a holistic view of primary education development and seeks to operationalise the strategy of UPE through district specific planning with emphasis on decentralised management, participatory processes, empowerment and capacity building at all levels. The programme is implemented through state level registered societies.

Aims of DPEP. The programmes aim at providing access to primary education for all children, reducing primary drop-out rates to less than 10 per cent, increasing learning achievement of primary schools students by 25 per cent and reducing the gender and social gap to less than five per cent. The programme is structured to provide additional inputs over and above the central/ state schemes for elementary education.

DPEP Programme Components

— Construction of classroom

— Appointment of new teachers

— Setting up of Early Childhood Education Centres (ECCE)

— Strengthening of SCERTS (State Council of Educational Research and Training)

— Setting up of Block Resource Centres/Cluster Resource Centre

— Teacher training

— Development of teaching learning materials

— Research

— Girl's education

— Education of SC and ST

— Education of disabled

— Distance education for Teacher's Training.

Unit of Programme Implementation. District is taken as a unit for programme implementation on the two point criteria:

* Education backwardness with female literacy below the national average.

* Districts with success in Total Literacy Campaigns (TLCS).
* Finance: Sharing of Expenditure
* DPEP is a Centrally sponsored scheme. Eighty five per cent of the expenditure on the project is met out by Central Govt. and 15% by State Govt. The grant is to be passed on to State Implementation Societies.
* Area Covered : Figures

  Initially in 1994, programme was launched in 42 districts of seven States.
* According to figures up to 2001, 219 districts have been covered in 15 States (Assam, Haryana, Karnataka, Kerala, Maharashtra, Tamil Nadu, Madhya Pradesh, Gujarat, Himachal Pradesh, Orissa, Andhra Pradesh, West Bengal, UP, Rajasthan and Bihar).

Lok Jumbish

* It is a special project in Rajasthan based upon people's movement for education for all. This is known as *"Lok Jumbish"*.
* This project has been supported by Swedish International Development Authority (SIDA)
* Aim of the project is "Education for All" through mobilisation and participation of people of Rajasthan in the education of children.
* Seventy five blocks have been covered from 1976-98.
* Preparation of Instructional Materials.
* Text books were developed for classes I-IV. The aim of the text books was achievement of Minimum Level of Learning (MLL).

Mid-day Meal Scheme

* Mid-day meal scheme was launched on 15 August, 1995 for the purpose of improving enrolment, attendance, and retention and improvement of nutritional status of students at this level.
* Cooked meal / processed food is supplied to children of classes I-V in all Government, local body and government-aided primary schools.

* During 1999-2000,9.90 crore children studying in 6.88 lakh schools were covered.
* Allocation of fund for 2000-01 was 1,090 crore.
* Central assistance is there for reimbursement of the cost of foodgrain and transportation charges, salaries of cook, helpers, construction of kitchen sheds.
* Where there is no provision for cooked meal /1 processed food, every child is provided 3 kg foodgrain (wheat / rice)

QUESTIONS

1. What do you mean by equality and equity in education ? Describe its need and importance with specific reference to India.
2. Describe the quality and equity in education with reference to various level of formal education in India.
3. Describe the steps to remove disparities in the provision of educational opportunities in India.
4. What you mean by weaker section of the society, Discuss briefly all aspects of developments in this contexts.
5. Discuss the education of scheduled castes and tribes as one of the weaker sections of the society.

14

Education for Adults

As a problem, Adult education was pointed out by the Indian Education Commission (1964-66). According to the Commission, even adult citizen in India is to be provided an opportunity for education of the type he wishes and which he should have for his personal enrichment; professional advancement and affective participation in social and political life. Three major components of adult education are taken into consideration literacy, functionality and social awareness. Sincere efforts are being undertaken in the free India since then. The National Policy on Education (1968) considered the recommendations of Indian Education Commission (1964-66). The National Adult Education Programme was launched on 2nd October, 1978 with the objective to provide literacy, functional skills and awareness among adult population of the age group of 15-35 years. National Policy of Education (1984) also took specific steps for adult education mass literacy programmes were undertaken. Teachers and students were involved. Centres for continuing education were set up in rural areas. Adequate instructional material was prepared. Efforts only at the Government levels can not solve this major problem. People should realise its significance and involve themselves. "Each one teach one" is the principle we should follow and the strong mass movement alongwith efforts at the Government level can find solution of the problem. The present chapter deals with some important features of adult education in the free India.

Eradication of Illiteracy

John Dewey states, "Education is life, education is growth and education is social process." Indian Constitution guarantees democracy and equality to every Indian citizen. Without literacy and education of masses, it is not possible to achieve the goal of democracy and equality. There is a little progress in this direction at present. The percentages of litracy in India has improved from 16.7 per cent in 1951 to 55.11 per cent in 1991. Adult literacy was given special attention during the last two decades. Administrative and technical resources have been established and voluntary agencies have been involved in large numbers.

The UGC. has suggested the following methods for the eradication of illiteracy:

1. Planned involvement of student and teachers.
2. Leadership role of universities and colleges in the mass programmes for functional literacy.
3. Re-orienting and developing education system for the development of students as well as community.
4. Extending human and physical resources of the universities in meeting urgent challengs of national reconstruction including eradication of iliteracy.

The strategies planned for mass participation of students and teacher felt by the U.G.C. are as follows :

(1) Centre based participation.

(2) Each one teach one/two/five/family.

(3) Motivational awareness campaign.

(4) Literacy material support.

Definitions : Literacy

For statistical purpose, UNESCO recommends the following definitions regarding illiteracy and adult literacy:

Literate. Literate is a person who can with understanding both read and write a short simple statement on his every day life.

Illiterate. Illiterate is a person who cannot with understanding both read the write a short simple statement on his every day life.

Functionally Literate. Functionally literate is a person who can engage in all those activities in which literacy is required for effective Functioning of his group and community and also for enabling him to continue to use reading, writing and calcuclation for his own and the community's development.

Functionally Illiterate. Functionally illiterate is a person who cannot engage in all those activities in which literacy is required for effective functioning of his group and community.

Adult Literacy. Adult literacy means teaching literates three Rs so that they may function meaningfully in their socio-economic and political setting.

Neo-Literates. Neo-literates are those persons who have attained a limited level of literacy mainly because they have not completed elementary school and might easily replapse into literacy if there are no appropriate reading materials for them.

Meaning of Adult Education

Morgan and Holmes. Adult education may be thought as the conscious effort of mature person to learn something new.

Bryson. Adult education includes all activities with educational purpose carried on in ordinary business of life by people who use only part of their energy to acquire intellectual development.

S.N. Mukerjee. Adult education may be defined as to include all instructions, formal and informal imparted to adults.

Ernest-Baker. Adult education is education given on part-time basis and given, therefore, concurrently with work and the earning of a living.

Reense. Fenster andHoule. Adult education may be concerned with any or more of three aspects of an individual' life: his work life, his personal life and his life a s citizen.

UNESCO. According to the UNESCO the term, "adult education" denotes the entire body of organised educational processes, whatever content level and method, whether formal or otherwise, whether they prolong or replace initial education in schools, colleges and universities as well as in apprenticeship, where by persons regarded as adults by the society to which they belong develop their abilites, enrich their knowledge, improve their technical or professional qualifications and bring about changes in their attitude or behaviour in the two fold perspective of full personnel development and participation in balanced and independent social, economic and cultural development. Adult education embraces all forms of educative experiences needed by men and women according to their varied interests and requirements, as their differing levels of comprehension and ability and in their changing roles and responsibilities throughout life."

The definition given by the UNESCO gives a total picture to adult education.

Components of Adult Education

Following are the three components of adult education:

1. Literacy
2. Functionality
3. Social Awareness.

Literacy. Literacy involves developing skills in reading, writing and numeracy.

Functionality. Functionality aims at relating one's learning experience to the activities engaged in so that one's work can be better managed. It also includes acquisition of additional skills to supplement one's income through productive activities.

Social Awareness. Social awareness includes senstivity to the impediments to development, about laws and government policies, and the need for the poor to organise themselves in pursuit of legitimate interests for group action.

The above mentioned components of adult education point out that adult education should be:

1. relevant to environment and learner's needs;
2. flexible regarding duration, time, location, instructional arrangements etc;
3. diversified curriculum, teaching and learning meterials and methods and
4. systematic in all respects of organisation.

Problem of Illiteracy. India's share of the world illiterate population in the age group of 15 and above is projected to increase from one fourth in 1980 to approximately one-third of the world's illiterates by 2000 A.D. According to 1981 Census, 107 millions of people in the age group of 15-35 are illiterate.

The literacy details based upon the Census of (1951, 1961, 1971, 1981 and 1991.)

	1951	*1961*	*1971*	*1981*	*1991*
Men	24.9	34.4	39.5	47.2	63.86
Women	7.9	12.9	18.5	25.0	39.42
Total	16.67	24.0	29.35	36.27	52.11

Problem of Production and Economic Growth. Adult stage is most important stage in human life. In this stage the person fully participates in different walks of life. Social and community relations depend upon these people. Production and economic growth are also affected by these people. Productivity and economic growth are affected seriously due to illiterate adults.

Problem of Development of Democratic Values. Indian Constitution guarantees democracy and equality to every citizen of the country. Without education the provisions of Indian Constitution cannot be achieved. People cannot participate in democratic process effectively due to lack of education. We may be unaware of our civil rights and duties due to lack of education. Adult education is important to develop awareness about civic right.

Problem of Joyous and Happy Living. Ignorance is the cause of the sufferings. Education through non-formal means makes one's life happy and joyful.

Problem of Universalisation of Education. Adult education through non-formal means can contribute significantly to solving the problem of universalisation of primary education. The efforts being made through formal system to solve the problem of universalisation of primary education are inadequate. We will have to depend upon non-formal and adult education programmes.

Problem of Improving their Proficiency and Skills: Motivation is the requisite condition for learning. Adult education programmes are motivating adults to participate actively in adult education programmes. This is improving their proficiency and skills.

Adult Literacy Develops New Hopes among Adults in their Lives. Education shows the direction for growth and development. New directions are sensed as a result of education. One feels better and prospersous future. Thus adult education develops new hopes among illiterate adults.

Efforts after Independence towards Adult Education

Indian Education Commission (1964-66). The Indian Education Commission (1964-66) for the first time highlighted the role of adult education and felt that it should be possible to eradicate illiteracy by 1985-86. The Commission viewed that adult education in a democracy is to provide every adult citizen with an opportunity for education of the type he wishes and which he should have for his personal enrichment, professional advancement and effective participation in social and political life. It also realised the importance of adult education for country's development. The Commission stressed the need of participation of universities in adult education.

The National Policy on Education (1968). The National Policy on Education (1968) considered the recommendations of the Indian Education Commission and the policy emphasized the significance of education not only for democratic participation but for production also, especially in agriculture. It also recommended the following: teachers and students should be actively involved as a pan of social and national programme; and people should be made functionally literate.

Many central schemes were started, for instance, Farmer's Functional Literacy Programme (1967-68) and Non-Formal Education for age group 15-35 (1975). The National Policy on Education (1968) asserted that highest priority should be given to adult education and universalisation of education.

The National Adult Education Programme (NAEP) was launched on 2nd October, 1978, with the objective of providing : literacy; functional skills; and awareness among illiterate adult population of the age group of 15-35 years. The National Adult Education Programme was included in the Sixth Year Plan (1980-85). Central Government funded rural functional literacy projects, voluntary agencies and universities. The State Resource Centres were established to work for the National Adult Education Programme.

National Policy on Education (1986). The National Policy on Education (1986) suggested the following important aspects of adult education:

(1) Mass Literacy Programmes.

(2) Large scale involvement of students and teachers.

(3) Centres in rural areas for continuing education. The Mass programme for Functional Literacy (MPFL) was organised since May, 1986, with the following objectives :

(a) To make literacy a people's mission.
(b) To harness all agencies for the mission.
(c) To mass literacy programmes as a challenge for the youth. To achieve the above objectives, the following steps should be taken to involve teachers and students of universities and colleges:
(i) Stressing functional literacy in National Service-Scheme (NCC).
(ii) Increasing coverage of student volunteers.
(iii) Specific projects should be taken up by students as a part of work-experience for scoial/national service and it should be included in their final results.
(iv) Provision for incentives for eradication of illiteracy.

Instructional Materials

Preparation of Instructional Materials. Instructional materials for adult education are different as compared with the that for the students of formal system of education. Materials are to be prepared for illiterates and neo-literates. The neo-illiterate refers to those who have not been enrolled in any school or literacy class and, therefore, have no literacy skills, while neo-literates are persons who have attained a limited level of literacy mainly because they have not completed elementary school, and might easily relapse into illiteracy if there are no appropriate reading materials for them.

The following steps are followed for preparing instructional material for illiterates and neo-literates.

Collection and Analysis of the Data Concerning the Problems of the Target Group. A field survey should be done to identify the problems and needs of the target group. It is required because materials to be prepared should be based on and linked with learner's problems and needs to help them to improve their quality of life.

Following points should be kept in mind while having a survey :

* Identify survey goals.
* Identify target group.
* Identify survey method.
* Determine who is to carry out the survey.
* Prepare, compile and organise the data.

Selection of Theme and Format of Material. Theme is selected depending upon the survey and then format for material is decided. Materials can be in the form of a booklet, pamphlet, poster, game, audio-visual medium, etc. Possible formats for materials are shown in here.

Possible Formats for Materials on Adult Education and Adult Literacy

Category	*Format*
Printed Book	Book, booklet, comic, etc.
Printed Non-book	Poster, leaflet (flyers), news periodicals, journals, flipchan, picture story-telling, hardboard set, card (flash cards, picture cards, etc.)
Electronics Media	Films (8 mm, 16 mm, etc.) movies, video slides, tapes, radio and T.V. programmes.
Games and Others	Conventional games, card games, puzzles, games of finance, board games simulation games puppet show, folk dance, songs, etc.

Procedure for Developing Instructional Materials. After deciding the theme and format of the material to be produced, the practical steps of material development such as preparation and drafting of manuscripts and illustrations, pretesting, etc., will strart. The steps of material preparation are shown in Figure.

Procedure for the development of instructional materials

Topic Selection
↓
Content Arrangement
↓
Script Preparation
↓
Illustration
↓
Arrangement and Editing
↓
Finalization of Title and Captions
↓
Field Test
↓
Revision
↓
Mass Production
↓
Distribution of Materials

Distribution of Instructional Material. Distribution of materials can be done by using the following ways :

(1) Free distribution by the Government.

(2) Rural libraries, adult education centres, community centres, religious places, recreational centres, tea stalls, etc.

(3) Mobile libraries.

(4) Mailing for remote areas.

(5) Wholesalers and retailers

Agencies for Promotion of Adult and Continuing Education

The following agencies are contributing to the promotion of adult and continuing education:

(1) The Directorate of Adult Education, Government of India, New Delhi.

(2) The Nehru Yuvak Kendras

(3) Voluntary Organisations.

(4) N.S.S., Bharat Vigyan Jatha, etc.

(5) The National Literacy Mission.

(6) Universities.

(7) The State and Central Government.

(8) The Indian Association of Adult and Continuing Education, New Delhi.

Universities have been re-organised to play the most important role in adult education. The University Grants Commission (U.G.C.) considered to provide assistance to the Universities for this purpose right from the fourth Five-Year Plan. The Commission agreed to implement the adult education through universities. The objective was bring these institutions closer to community through on-going programmes, viz. Functional Literacy; Non-formal Education for youth in the age group of 15-35 years; and follow-up reading service for neo-literate adults.

Objectives of Adult and Continuing Education and Extension : U.G.C.

The U.G.C. framed the following objectives for Adult and Continuing Education and Extension:

1. To enable universities to establish the necessary linkage with community.

2. To provide opportunities for disseminating knowledge in all walks of life.

Literacy and Economical Survival. Literacy is also a tool for economical survival. Literacy increases the effectiveness of all transactions made by the literate in his or her economic environment. Without literacy, it is impossible to survive in relation to today's economic institutions.

Literacy and Social Survival. Social survival means self-esteem, a sense of belonging, opportunities for an authentic expression of personal values with a release from the tyranny of social institutions. Literacy has indeed released from the burden of inferiority. Literacy has changed the social psychology of the family and checked certain social evils like suicide, drug abuse, crime, teenage marriage, etc.

Literacy and Political Survival. An illiterate person feels difficulties regarding political life. He/she has to become the follower of literates. In many countries, the right to vote is denied due to illiteracy. Literacy makes democracy possible.

Literacy and Cultural Survival. Cultures cannot be perpetuated longer through oracy. Oral cultures are fast disappearing. Literacy is the most important instrument of ethnic and cultural pride and social solidarity.

Literacy and the Survival of the Species. Only the literates are likely to have peace and disarmament as part of their individual agenda for a better world. Thus, in the universalisation of literacy, there are implications for the survival of the species. Literates can understand the problems like population explosion, protection of the environment, the nuclear threat, disarmament and peace, etc.

National Literacy Mission (1987)

Spread of literacy has been an important programme since Independence. The percentage of literacy has improved from 16.7 pert cent in 1951 to 55.11 per cent in 1991.However, despite the efforts af the universalisation of primary education and adult education in the past, the number of illiterates have progressively increased from 300 million in 1951 to 437 million in 1981.

Adult literacy, therefore, received special attention during the last ten years. Administrative and technical resource structures have been established and voluntary agencies have been involved in large numbers. Ministry of Human Resource Development in collaboration with Universities, Colleges and other agencies and organisations launched the National Literacy Mission in 1987 with an ambitious plan of covering 30 million by 1990 and an additional 50 millions by 1995 and organisation of continuing programmes through *Jana Shikshan Nilayama* (JNS). The following objectives have been specified by National Literacy Mission :

(1) Achieve self-reliance in literacy and numeracy.

(2) Become aware of causes of deprivation.

(3) Acquire skills to enable adult to improve their economic status.

(4) Cultivation of the values of national integration, conservation of the environment, women's equality, observance of small family norms, etc.

To achieve the above objectives, the following suggestions have been made:

(1) Securing people's participation.

(2) Launching mass movement.

(3) Significant involvement of universities.

Total Literacy Campaign in India (TLC-1990)

According to decisions of UNESCO's General Conference and Executive Board, we are to enter the 21st century as an illiteracy free world. This goal was appreciated in 1988 by 21 Governments of Member States and four International Non-Governmental Organisations.

UNESCO had evolved a Plan of Action to help member States in all regions of the world to eradicate illiteracy by the year 2000. The ten year period (1990-2000) emerged as the International Decade for Literacy during which not only illiterates would be made literate but also they would be kept literate. This necessitates restructuring the existing ones and setting up new structures whenever needed at village, town, and district levels during the decade so that those who have been made literate can use literacy in their daily lives through reading, writing, discussing and making other communities.

The above total literacy campagin by UNESCO helped to achieve the objective of literacy for all by 2000 AD which has been mentioned in the National Policy on Education-1986 and enunciated in the Programme of Action-1986.

Suggestions for the Improvement of Adult Literacy

1. Motivation of adult learners is a must.

2. Use of specific methodologies for teaching adults. For example :

   (1) Laubach Method. In this method adults are taught by showing pictures form, charts representing various words.

   (2) Synthetic Method. Synthesis means combination of two or more words. In this method, letters are learnt individually and then are combined into words.

(3) Analytical Method. In this method learners are taught through words by disjoining them.

3. Programmes should be organised for imparting training to adult literacy functionaries. The state resource centres of the states can be involved in these programmes.

4. Good instructional materials should be developed and be distributed free of cost at various adult literacy centres.

5. More funds should be allocated by the States and the Centre for the purpose of adult literacy. There should be regular monitoring and evaluation of the programmes of adult literacy.

Non-Formal Education : Meaning

C.L. Kundu. Formal, non-formal and informal education are conceived today not as alternatives but as complementary activities of a single system. Adult education is treated as a part of total non-formal education.

Coombs (1977). Non-formal education is any organised learning activity outside the structure of the formal education that is consciously aimed at meeting specific learning needs.

Coombs and Manzoor. Non-formal education is the organised and semi-organised educational activity operating outside the regular structure and routines of the formal system. It is aimed at serving a great variety of learning needs of different sub-groups in the population, both young and old

Adiseshiah. Non-formal education is wide ranging because it comprehends all learning outside the formal system and has no parameters of time and space. It can be classified for pre-school, unschooled and underschooled children in the age group 1-15 and for youth and adults: (unschooled, schooled or needing new additional skills) in the age group 15-60.

Characteristics

1. It is a life long continuous process of learning.
2. Learning is integrated with life, work and environment.
3. It is flexible and open-ended as regards to syllabus, textbooks and class management.

4. Time, place, duration, learning methods and materials are shaped according to the needs and convenience of the learners.

5. It has flexible points of entry and exit and re-entry and re-exit.

6. It is based upon the principle of maximisation of human potential.

7. It is multifaceted process.

8. It prepares for active life and effective work.

Characteristics (Programme of Action 1986)

Characteristics of non-formal education mentioned in the Programme of Action-1986 are listed below (Mohanty, 1992 p. 132)

1. A learner approach with instructor as a facilitator.
2. Emphasis on learning rather than teaching.
3. Organisation of activities to enable learners to progress at their own pace.
4. Use of efficient techniques to ensure fast pace of learning.
5. Stress on continuous learner's evaluation and certification.
6. Scholastic achievements, particularly language and Maths as per norms of the formal system.
7. Creation of participatory learning environment.
8. Organisation of joyful extra-curricular activities including singing, dancing, plays, games sports etc.
9. Ensuring all facilities and incentives to girls and children of SC/ST and others.
10. The instructors being local are acceptable to this community. These should be preferably from weaker sections.

Target Groups

Target groups for non-formal education are all age groups and sections of society: children, youth and old.

1. In the beginning, non-formal education was meant only for drop-outs who left schools in the end of the session or at end, without completing the course.

2. Now it is intended for all who have left schools or have not entered into schools at all, i.e. non-formal education is sought to cater to the elementary education needs of all sections of the society belonging to different age groups and professional groups or individuals so for not engaged to any work or service. Individuals who have been cut off from the stream of formal education can be divided into two groups:

   1. 6-14 yrs. age group

   2. 15-35 yrs. age group.

   Children in the age group 6-14 yrs fall into two categories :

   (1) Those who have never seen a school; (2) Those who have attended school for a short time. The syllabus for the age group 6-14 yrs- should consist of knowledge related to language, mathematics, environment and vocational knowledge. There should be continuous evaluation and there should be no formal examination. The individual of age group 15-35 should improve their efficiency and vocational skills besides proficiency in reading, writing and numeracy.

3. Non-formal education covers levels of education ranging from pre-primary to university education.

4. Non-formal education rather recently gone farther to cover the field of higher education. Open university education or any kind of correspondence education or distance education is the example of non-formal education in the higher education.

5. Non-formal education can include within school education other kinds of professional and vocational programmes like community development farming, agricultural extension, technical training. Such education is meant for children, youths and adults for whom formal education has either been unsuitable or unfavourable. It is more flexible in structure, curriculum, organisation and evaluation.

Education and Mass Illiteracy

The Problem of Mass Illiteracy. The problem of mass illiteracy is a significant one. According to K.G. Saiyidain: "If someone were to prepare a literacy map of the world and colour the illiterate areas of the earth black, India will, to our shame look like a dark continent." This remark by one of India's leading educationists highlights the need for educating the hitherto ignorant masses so that they are able to understand the real meaning of freedom and make adequate contribution towards national development.

India's efforts towards universalisation of education, advancement of higher learning and technical education, coupled with programmes of national development, have been impressive. In the world today only those nations are economically backward which have a low literacy percentage. Almost all the advanced nations of the world have wiped out illiteracy from their land. In fact, their economic growth owes much to this factor. These nations realised the importance of mass literacy quite early in their schemes of development and achieved the target through their concerted efforts in this direction. India, too, needs concerted efforts in this regard.

Overview of Past Efforts and Present Position. Let us consider the data covering the period 1951 to 1988. The number of educational institutions and pupils have registered a phenomenal increase. During this period, the number of primary schools was up from 209671 to 543677; higher secondary schools from 7288 to 66857; colleges from 498 to 4329 and professional training institutions (medical, engineering, agricultural colleges) etc. from 155 to 876. We had 142 full-fledged universities in 1988 compared to just 27 in 1951.

Our efforts have borne fruits. The number of literates in the country in the first three decades since independence (till 1981) increased fourfolds, from 60 million to 247 million; but the number of illiterates has also increased, from 300 million to 431 million. The reason was that we had doubled our population in this period and that wiped out all advantages of extended educational facilities. As experts put it, we had to remain where we were.

Similarly, disparities between literacy rate between male and female population persisted, 47 per cent for the male but only 24.8 per cent for the female population; we were unable to give adequate attention to removal of regional disparities either; while 65 percent of Kerala's rural population became literate, only 5 percent of their counterparts in Rajasthan could read or write.

Causes of Illiteracy

Population Problem. The first major cause is our galloping population which turns all our efforts at development into an exercise of one step-forward-two steps-backward. It is really shocking that from 350 million in 1951 India will be registering an estimated 1000 million population by 2000 A.D.

Multiple Languages. India is a multilingual nation. There are varying regional concepts of priorities. This makes uniformity of approach for universalization of education a difficult task.

Multi-religious Society. Ours is a multi-religious society. In this society, religion plays a dominant role in social behaviour. Different sections have their own preference for educational structure and schooling system.

Disadvantaged Groups. There are many disadvantaged groups in our society e.g. school drop-outs, scheduled castes, scheduled tribes, working children, scattered and isolated communities in hilly areas. All these need speical effort and different approaches for propagation of education among them.

Measures to Arrest Mass Illiteracy

In order to arrest mass illiteracy, two measures are generally suggested by experts: (1) compulsory basic education for all children in the age-group 6-14; (2) functional literacy to all illiterate adults in the age group 15-35.

Education for All Children in the Age-group 6-14 Years. Article 45 of Directive Principles of State Policy in the Constitution of India clearly states that "That State shall endeavour to provide for, within a period often year from the commencement of this Constitution, free and compulsory education for all children till they complete the age of fourteen years." This provision was to be fulfilled by 1960, but when the deadline came, the fulfilment of the Constitutional provision seemed a distant dream. Now the 9th Five Year Plan has ended, we are not in a position to achieve 100% literacy. The one and the only reason is our galloping population which the farmers of our Constitution failed to visualise. Needless to add that the government has taken various measures to achieve the target.

Functional Literacy to All Illiterate Adults. The second measure is providing functional literacy to all adults.

National Literacy Mission. To meet the challenge of mass literacy and universal education, a number of programmes have been initiated by the Government. Eradication of Illiteracy has been recognised as one of the five national missions-National Literacy Mission-which seeks to impart literacy to illiterate adults in the age group 15-35.

The first phase of this programme covering 30 million adults was targetted to be achieved by 1990, mainly through the National Programme for Adult Literacy. This scheme was launched in 1978. Efforts were made to impart literacy and skill proficiency through various learning programmes which include Rural Functional Literacy Programme (RFLP), State Adult Education Programme (SAEP). Programmes were taken up by voluntary agencies like Nehru Yuva Kendras and by universities where students were involved in literacy work. By 1988-89 some 278 adult centres were set up with an approximate enrolment of nine million adults; 65 per cent of these centres are in what are recognised as educationally backward areas.

Unfortunately, the situation is still alarming.

Non-Formal Education. The programme of Non-Formal Education (NFE), also launched in the late seventies, is directed towards out-of-school children in the 9-14 age group including those who somehow failed to enter schools at all or dropped out before reaching the permanent literacy level. According to figures available, out of 100 children enrolled in primary classes, about 60 per cent stay in the school till class V, completing the essential basic education. However, once they cross into the upper primary, almost 85 per cent of them go on to complete the high school. The N.F.E. programme is picking up momentum. to more than 241000.

However, participation of girls in this programme remained low. The centres for girls were a few and parents hesitated in enrolling their adolescent daughters in co-educational centres. Now the proportion of N.F.E. centres for girls has gone up and the girls' participation in education has consequently increased. Another welcome move has been to adopt an area-based approach, offering facilities as per the feasibility and need of the communities served.

QUESTIONS

1. Define the term literate, illiterate and neo-literate. Briefly discuss various aspects of adult literacy with specific reference to India.
2. Discuss the efforts made in India after Independence towards adult education.
3. What is the difference between adult education and adult literacy ? How an illiteracy be eradicated from India ?
4. Comment upon the instructional materials and methods of teaching for use of the purpose of adult education and adult literacy ?
5. Comment upon the following:

   (a) Importance of Adult Literacy.

   (b) National Literacy Mission 1987

15

Distance Education

Educational Technology has been revolutionised by the Communication technology has revolutioned educationol technology. Today there are a number of media of instructional technology. These was a time when distance education was considered of lower quality, but time may come when people may prefer distance education modes for developing desired competencies. We today feel that both channels i.e. formal education and distance education (a non-formal means of education) are good. The choice depends upon our requirement. In case one is in service or living at a place where formal education services are not available one may go for distance education programmes. India has made significant progress in developing distance education for achieving the aim of "education for all." The present chapter deals with a few aspects on efforts made in india with specific reference to distance education.

Meaning of Distance Education

Non-formal education system is being utilised today alongwith formal education system. Distance education and open university education are the examples of non-formal education in higher education. According to Coombs (1977), non-formal education is any organised learning activity outside the structure of the formal education that is consciously aimed at meeting specific learning needs. Non-formal education is very flexible and open-ended as regards to syllabus/textbooks and class management. In this system time, place, duration lea[illegible]ng methods and materials are shaped according to the lea[illegible]ers. Non-formal education programme aims at realising the eduational objectives within a limited time span.

Distance education is a popular term for correspondence education. The terms correspondence education, distance education open education home study, postal tuition mean almost the same.

Education that is imparted from a distance. It may be called as remote control education. It is more that the scope of correspondence education as there is the use of multimedia instead of simple use of print media. We can say that the term 'Distance Education' is the evolved form of 'Correspondence Education' and open Education.

Evolutionary Nature of the Concept of Distance Education

1. Distance Education : Use of all types sophisticated communication teachnology.
2. Open Education : Use of multi-media (Radio, T.V.); contact programme and postal system.
3. Correspondence Education : Use of only postal system ; print media; contact programme
4. Formal Education : Schools, Colleges & Universities

A few definitions of distance education are mentioned below :

Peters : "Distance education is a method of indirect instruction , implying geographical and emotional separation of the teacher and the taught where as, in main-stream education the relationship between a teacher and students in the classroom is based upon social norms, in distance education it is based upon technological rules."

Jack Foks : "Distance education is a mode of learning with certain characteristics which distinguish it from the campus based mode of learning"

V. K. Kohli : "Distance education is a modern system of non-formal education. It can be described as correspondence education, open education, or open learning and characterised by relaxed entry qualification learning at one's own pace and convenience, freedom of choice of courses and use of appropriate communication technology."

Rameshwari Pandya, Shetal Zaveri and Bhanita Thakuria (2002-03)

Pandya and others in their article published in the I C T in Education (2002-2003), a publication of the Centre of Advanced Study in Education, Faculty of Education and Psychology. The M. S. university of Baroda, Vadouara, mention the following views on the concept of distance education:

"Distance teaching in its strict sense means the imparting of instruction through correspondence only. In such a system, one never comes face to face with one another. Only the postal services form a link between the teacher and the student. All the problems and difficulties of the students are solved through correspondence only."

Distance education has been defined as a method of teaching in which the teacher bears the responsibility of imparting knowledge and skill to a student who does not receive instructions orally, but who studies in a place and at distance determined by his individual circumstances. It is thus an individual method of instruction in which each student receives continuous individual attention and assistance to meet his special needs throughout the course.

Many people, however, use the term home study and correspondence course synonymously.

The origin of distance education can be traced back to the origin of postal services. This can be viewed on the basis of the contents of those letters that are of advisory in nature or full of suggestion. One is enhancing one's knowledge or solving one's problem with the support of the other through correspondence.

History of Distance Education : West

1. *Germany*. Charles Toussaint, French man started teaching languages through postal services in 1856.
2. *USA*. USA started international correspondence school of education for correspondence studies.
3. Australia-W.A, Grundy, a health inspector of Austial used correspondence education for imparting training to rural health inspectors in 1910.

4. USSR used correspondence education for imparting education at secondary and tertiary levels in 1947.

5. Netherlands-Correspondence education was implemented in 1947 for education of the masses.

6. U.K (The Great Britain)- Harold Wilson the leader of opposition in Britain gave the idea of Open University in 1963. First Open University in the U.K. was established in 1977. Other countries of the world also opened Open Universities.

Historical Background : India

1. University of Delhi-Directorate of Correspondence was set up in 1962. For the first time broadcast was used. Prof. Nurul Hassan, then Education Minister of India highlighted the significance of correspondence and open university education.

2. Punjabi University, Patiala-Punjabi University, Patiala was the second in the race to start correspondence education in 1967.

3. Examples of other universities who followed the experiments of Delhi & Patiala:

   (a) Mysore University (1969)

   (b) Panjab University, Chandigarh (1971)

   (c) Himachal Pradesh University Shimla (1971)

   Almost all the universities in India are now having correspondence units.

Problems

An International Seminar on "Distance Education: Experience of Open Universities" was organised by Indira Gandhi National Open University in 1985. The following problems and recommendations were pointed out:

1. Problem of identification of courses and development of relevant instructional material.

2. Problem of organisational structure of Open Universities.

3. Problem of use of mass-media.

4. Problem of norms for admission of students.
5. Problem of evaluation.
6. Problem of financing Open Universities.
7. Problems related to assignments, contact programmes and support services.

Bases/Rationale of Distance Education

Following points serve as the bases of distance education:

1. Education is a life long process.
2. One can learn at any stage of development.
3. Educational opportunities for all i.e "Education for all" irrespective of barriers of distance, age, time and place.
4. Meeting the psychological, intellectual, social, emotional etc. needs of leamfr/s.
5. Improvement of standard of living.
6. To increase production & consequently, economy of the country.
7. Equity and equality in education.

Kothari Commission (1964-66)

Provisions Required —

1. Provision of education to those who are not even in a postion to attend part time classes.
2. Provision of availability of the teaching staff in the existing institution for consultations of students.
3. Provision for radio broadcast and T.V telecast.
4. Provisions for special courses through correspondence (e.g industrial and agriculture) besides university and school education.
5. Provisions of courses that may promote cultural and aesthetic values.
6. Provisions of in-service training courses for in-service teacher education.

Merits

1. Availability of education at all levels of education.
2. Provision of professional and technical education alongwith liberal education /traditional edcuation.
3. Easy conditions of admission.
4. Flexibility in structure (no condition of place, time, etc.).
5. One can progress at his or her own speed or pace.
6. It is economical.
7. It suits all age group of people.
8. One can learn desired competencies and skills while at work or service.
9. In-service education to teachers & other professionals.
10. Achievements of constitutional provisions like equity and equality provision of education opportunities.
11. Educational and vocational guidance.
12. Extension activities.
13. Adult education.

Distance Education Universities

In India first Open University was established at Hyderabad (Andhra Pradesh) on 20th Agugust 1982. Indira Gandhi National Open University was established on 19th November, 1985. Dr. Ram Reddy was the founder Vice-chancellor of this University.

Following are a few examples of universities imparting distance education:

1. Indira Gandhi National Open Univerisity (IGNOU)
2. B.R. Ambedkar Open University, Hyderabad (Andhra Pradesh)
3. Kota Open University, Kota (Rajasthan)
4. Nalanda Open University (Bihar)
5. Yashwant Rao Chavan Maharashtra Open University, Nasik (Maharashtra)

6. Madhya Pradesh Bhoj Open University, Bhopal (Madhya Pradesh)
7. Ambedkar Open University Ahmedabad (Gujarat)
8. Karnataka State Open University, Mysore (Karnataka)
9. Netaji Subhash Open University, Calcutta (West Bengal)
10. Rajrishi Tandon Open University, Allahabad (Uttar Pradesh)

Components of Distance Education

1. Printed instructional materials
2. Assignments and response sheets
3. Personal contact programmes
4. Audio-Visual multi-media, educational technology communication technology
5. Study Centres (Accredited Centres)

Salient Features of Distance Education

1. Distance education or learning is primarily a self-learning method.
2. The student has to depend more on his own initiative and motivation than anything else.
3. Education is imparted to distant or off campus students.
4. It is quite innovative, flexible, and less expensive.
5. The learner progresses according to his own capacity. Nothing is imposed from outside and everything is achieved by himself. That is why, this system is psychologically as well as sociologically sound and effective.
6. Distance education system is considered democratic as millions of people all over the world are able to fulfil their academic aspirations and satisfy their unfulfilled desires of knowledge through this system.
7. This system is psychologically as well as sociologically sound and effective.

8. Distance education has been able to equalise educational opportunities among the people irrespective of their status and conditions. It is assuming socialistic dimensions.
9. Home study or correspondence method no doubt lacks the inspiring contact with the teacher but inspiring teachers are rare and in correspondence study the adult has a strong motivation to learn.
10. Contact courses and study centres are provided in the distance' education.
11. Distance education system is supported with suitable radio and television programme alongwith print media (assignments and printed lessons) Programmed learning or programmed instruction is also used for slow learners.
12. Open University is an example of distance education system.
13. Distance education should not be confined to merely helping students to get university degrees but it should be used for helping workers in industry, commerce and agriculture to improve their competence and increase productivity.
14. Distance education can promote the aesthetic cultural and intellectual standards of the people. Some people desire to enrich their lives by studying subjects of cultural and aesthetic value like art, appreciation, liberally criticism, philosophy, languages etc.

Aims of Distance Education

1. To advance and disseminate learning and knowledge by a diversity of means, including the use of any communication technology.
2. To promote the educational well-being of the community.
3. To encourage the Open University and distance education system in the education pattern of a nation.
4. To co-ordinate and determine the standard in the system.
5. To reverse the tide to admission in formal institutions.

6. To offer education to people in their own homes and at their own jobs.
7. To enable the students to earn while they learn.
8. To provide counselling and guidance to people.
9. To take education to remote areas like deserts, hills etc, through radio, television and correspondance.

National Policy on Education Aims of Open Education:

1. Open University system should act as instrument for democratising education.
2. Provision of educational opportunites at the higher education level.
3. Making education, a life long process through open education at all levels.

Targets :

Programme of Action

1. Increase in enrolment up to 16.5% at the end of eighth plan.
2. Cost-effectiveness in education through various strategies.

International Seminar on Distance Education-1985

1. **Problem of Identification of Courses and Development of Instructional Materials**
   1. Courses should be for traditional education, adult education, vocational education, etc.
   2. Special courses for women, and backward sections of society.
   3. Team approach should be followed for developing instructional metrials.
   4. Bridge courses should be developed for students to enable them to come to the average standard.
2. **Problem of Organisational Structure of the University**
   1. Two types of organisation structure of University was proposed :

* Centrally controlled structure and

* Autonomous institutions.

2. There should be three operational wings :

* Educational or course production division

* Student services or support services

* General or administrative wings

3. Problems of Admission. Admission should be made in open universities taking into consideration that open universities are to provide education to all. Special emphasis is given to working people, house-wives, drop-outs, handicapped, and other disadvantaged sections of society. Norms for admission to open universities should be flexible and liberal in comparison to those in conventional universities. Special consideration should be given in the case of admission of physically handicapped persons.

4. Problem of Evaluation. Evaluation of students should be done on the basis of continuous assessment through projects, traditional examinations, computer-assisted learning, question banks, etc.

5. Problem of Finance. Adequate support from Central and State governments is needed. Self-financing will affect the quality.

6. Problems Related to Assignments, Contact Programmes and Support Services. There should be regular submission and evaluation of student assignments. Contact programmes should be of short duration. Support services (student services) should be a must for an Open University.

Information Technology and Quality of Distance Education

1. The Three Information Worlds. Today information centres/ worlds can be categorised into three :

(a) Literature world of Libraries and Archives.

(b) Document World of information centres, clearing houses documentation centres and record centres.

(c) Data World of Computers. Information should collected from computers, telecommunication and automated information system.

2. **To Quote Pandyation (2002-03).** "The student of 2010 may not even walk into a asroom as many colleges and universities are experimenting with satellite admissions and have worked dormitories to campus-wide data networks "The student can research on a library's electronic database, file assigime us directly into his professor's compute . check class schedules, conduct bank transactions and other jobs. Afacult member on the other hand can monitor the students's progress and share his views with other colleagues. The PCs will also help to bring together ideas, learning experiences, notes and research papers, computers not only control the robots but will be entering into an era of computer integrated manufacturing."

3. **To Quote Prof. M. Mukhopadhyaya.** Chairman National Open School, on the concluding day of the three-day international conference-cum-meeting on "Electronic information for distance education" held in New Delhi.

"The cost of having electronic information technology for distance education may be very high, but think of the 'cost' if we do not have it."

The importance of information technology for the improvement in the equality of distance education is pointed out by prof Mukhopadhya. Following are the highlights of the conference-cum-meeting.

Development of Working Agenda. The viability and feasibility of electronic information technology for open schools in developing countries, sharing of capabilities, experiences and expertise in electronic imformation technology and the use of this technology in distance education in respective countries were included in the agenda.

Development of Action Plans. Action plans were prepared for Introducing electronic information technology in learning, planning and management of open learning.

Pooling of Experiences. Experiences of different countries should be pooled and utilised too for the benefit of all the member countries.

Policy and Strategy to Involve Tele-communication in Distance Education. Tele-communication should be used in distance education.

QUESTIONS

1. What do you mean by distance education ? Discuss the bases of the distance education.
2. Comment upon the historical background of distance education.
3. Comment upon the following :

   (a) Distance education universities in India.

   (b) Information Technology and distance education.
4. Describe salient features of distance education.
5. Comment upon the following :

   (a) Aims of distance education

   (b) Problems of distnace education.
6. Describe recommendations of various commission/committees/National Policy on Education regarding distance education in India.

16

Controlling the Quality

In Inida, history of higher education can be traced back to Ancient India. Universities like Taxilla University and Nalanda University were world famous ones. The material as well as religious education was of high quality. Muslim education was of good quality but centres of higher education were not much. British period again contributed towards higher education by opening universities at Bombay, Madras and Calcutta in 1857. The scenario after independence was altogether different. Growth and development of higher education after independence is remarkable. Emphasis is given to improvement of standards. Various commissions/ committees recommended steps for quality control. This chapter deals briefly various aspects of higher education with specific reference to quality control.

Pre-Independence Period

Buddhist Education Universities. Buddhist education system (200 BC to 200 AD) was founded by Lord Gautama Buddha of the Sakayas. There were a number of centres of higher education. A few famous names of universities are Taxilla University, Nalanda University, Ballabhi University, Vikramshila University, Mithila University, etc. The curricular areas were: The Vedas, Vedanta, Grammar Ayurveda, Military Science, Astrology, Agriculture, Commerce, Politics, Diplomacy, Logic, Philosophy, Tantra Vidya, Nyaya Philosophy etc Scholarly debates were encouraged. Discussion method, question-answer method, oral methods, and other procedures were used for teaching the contents.

Establishment of First three Universities at Bombay, Madras and Calcutta in 1857. In 1853, the British Parliament for the first time instituted an inquiry into the educational system and it was as a consequence of this step that the famous Wood's Despatch of 1854 proposed the establishment of afiliating universities on the model of London University, which led to the setting up of the universities at Bombay, Madras and Calcutta in 1857.

1900-1947 (Universities in India). At the time of independence, there were about fifty universities.

Post-Independence Period

Explosion in the Number of Universities. The number of universities and colleges increased significantly.

Structure of Higher Education. Organisational structure of higher education is the result of contribution f various Commission or Committees :

(1) Radhakrishnan Commission (1948).

(2) Committee on Model Act for Universities under the Chairmanship of Prof. D.S Kothari in 1961.

(3) Education Commission (1964-66)

(4) Committee on Governance of universities and colleges in 1969 under the chairmanship of Dr. P.B. Gajendragadkar.

(5) The CABE Committee on educational structure and vocationalisation 1972.

(6) In the National Policy on Education (1986) the basic thrust was on human resource development, keeping in view the challenge of 21st century. Programme of Action was brought out.

(7) Review Committee was set up in 1990. The focus was towards an enlightened and human society. Three points were emphasized: right to work; unity and integrity of the nation; and impoverishment of the inner man.

(8) New education policies are coming up at the state level, e.g. New education Policy (2000) Haryana.

Aims and Objectives of Higher Education in India

University Education Commission—(1948-49). University Education Commission (Radhakrishnan Commission) mentioned the following aims and objectives of higher education :

1. Providing healthy representation in politics, administration, profession, industry and commerce in the changing political, social and economic conditions.
2. Developing an intellectual attitude towards things and encouraging growth of knowledge among the youth in the universities.
3. Emphasizing social reform through the creation of foresightedness, intelligence and courageous leadership.
4. Encouraging universities to play their part as organs of culture and the intellectual leaders.
5. Make an endeavour for the success of democracy.
6. Discovering the innate qualities of individuals and developing them through suitable training.
7. Promoting social emancipation.
8. Creating the sentiments of national discipline, intellectual-awareness, intellectual development, justice, freedom, equality and brotherhood.

Education Commission (1964-66)

1. To seek and cultivate new knowledge, to engage, vigorously and fearlessly in the pursuit of truth and to interpret old knowledge and beliefs to the light of new needs and discoveries.
2. To provide the right kind of leadership in all walks of life, to identify gifted youth and help them develop their potential to the foil by evaluating physical fitness, development of powers of the mind and cultivating right interests, attitudes and moral and intellectual values.
3. To provide society with competent men and women trained in agriculture, arts, medicine, science and technology, with a sense of social purpose.
4. To strive to promote equality and social justice and to reduce social and cultural differences through diffusion of education; and
5. To foster in the teachers and students, and through them in society generally, the attitudes and values needed for developing the good life in individuals and society.

National Policy on Education—(1986). According of National Policy on Education (1986) objectives and importance of higher education are stated below:

1. Higher education provides people with an opportunity to reflect on the critical, social, economic, cultural, moral and spiritual issues facing humanity.
2. It contributes to national development through disssemination of specialised knowledge and skills. It is, therefore, a crucial factor for survival. Being at the apex of the educational pyramid, it has also a key role in producing teachers for the education system.
3. Higher education in India will have to adopt and promote the values of democracy, egalitarianism, social justice, and secularism.
4. It must emphasize excellence, high performance and problem solving.
5. As a mechanism of socialization it should prepare the generation under the charge for a new design for living—a design aimed at promoting a'quality of life that is desirable, feasible and sustainable.

Steps in Quality Control in Higher Education

Recommendations of Radhakrishnan Commission (1948-49)

1. A university degree should not be required for Government administrative services. Special state examination for recruitment to the various services should be organised.
2. No credit is given, at present for class work in courses except sometimes in the case of practical work such credit should be given.
3. Three years will be involved for the first degree.
4. The standards for success at the examination should as far as possible be uniform in various universities and should be raised. We suggest a candidate should get 70 per cent or more marks to secure a first class, 55 per cent to 69 per cent for a second and at least 40 per cent for a third.

National Policy on Education (1986). According to National Policy on Education (1986), following steps are recommended for quality control in higher education :

1. Urgent steps should be taken to protect the system from degradation.
2. Establishment of autonomous colleges.
3. The creation of autonomous departments within universities on a selective basis.
4. Redesigning the courses and programmes to meet the demands of specialisation.
5. Decentralisation of academic administration.
6. Promotion of creativity, innovation and higher standards.
7. Establishment of Council of Higher Education for state level planning and co-ordination of higher education.
8. Making provision for minimum facilities.
9. Regulating admission according to capacity.
10. Systemetic assessement of teacher's performance.
11. Providing enhanced research and ensuring its high quality.
12. Co-ordination and developing inter-disciplinary research.
13. Establishing rural universities.

Steps for Quality Control in the Near Future : India. The review of the literature on quality control in higher education reveals that following steps should be taken in the near future with specific reference to India:

Understanding the Current Trends in Higher Education

* **Trend to Use of Planning Technologies.** Planning technologies are being used today to protect higher education system from degradation. We have seen that in India educational planners have realised the significance of planning & we are using current planning technologies.
* **Trend to Consider Education as an Investment Sector.** Today, educational planners consider education as an investment sector to improve and increase human capital

& provide manpower requirement of the country. There is a need to develop a mechanism thay may regulate the demand and supply in the employment market. Imbalances in this mechanism are to be screened out. Cost effectiveness of the system is also to be assessed.

* **Trend to Ensure the Equal Distribution of Educational Facilities.** The education of masses is linked with economic development. It is to be ensured that the distribution is equal to all sections of the society.

Mass Media and Computer Technology. Presently, computers have entered our educational institutions. That is why, there is a need for changing the outlook of the existing staff.

Use of Diversified Structures to Meet the Needs the Changing Needs of Skills. Job requirements have caused changes in syllabi, methods, educational technology. This is a need to develop diversified structures to develop required skill in the market.

International Co-operation. Innovations or new model of education can be developed through sharing of experiences with other countries. There is a need of international cooperation.

Liaison with Industry. Liaison with industry is to be increased. Concept like "faculty of the future" and "future class rooms" should be kept in mind. Staff can be invited from the industry. Students can be given first hand experience at the work place in the society. Today, there is a big gap between the formal setting and real requirement of the work place, staff and students. This is important keeping in view the concept of life long teaming, the basic need of learning society.

Non-Formal Strategies. Education is not the need of our young boys and girls but also important for adults. Education is important for adults as reinforcement. Formal education has its limitations. It is performing its fundamental functions only. The educational needs with the changes with time can be met out only with the help of non-formal educational strategies. We must design such non-formal means of education that may perform development function throughout one's life. This will support them.

New Education Model. Education should contribute to the development of learning society. The socio-economic conditions should be taken into considerations. The education system should be so devised that quality education can be provided as a right for every one and not a privilege for just a few. Besides this the education system should also achieve the following goals/aims:

— Sensitising people to societal changes.

— Satisfaction of citizens and parents through accountability.

— Continuous development of structures that may meet the changing nee ds

— These structures should utilise the resources within the institution and outside the institution.

Quality in Higher Education : Arun Nigavekar

Professor Arun Nigavekar is a well known physicist and educationist. He is the present Chairman of UGC, India (July 16,2002). He has worked in area of decentralisation of UGC administration, quality education, higher education & self-sustainability and administrative reforms in governance of higher education. He is the recepient of certain awards like phia foundation award; UNESCO honour and Swami Vivekananda Award. He is the former vice- Chancellor, Pune University and former UGC member

Present Position on the Number of Higher Education Institutions in India

There are 296 institutes of higher education in India today (Jan, 2002) Central, State, deemed Universities, IITs, and institutes of national importance *e.g.* Sanjay Gandhi Medical Institute, Allahabad, Post Graduate Institute of Medical Education and Research, Chandigarh, Indian Institutes of Technology (IITs), Jawahar Lal Nehru University, Anna University and Pune University (It attracts 30% of foreign students) are the examples of first level institutions in India. Gokhale Institute of Policy & Economics. Pune, Jamia Millia Islamia. Delhi University, etc. are second level institutes in India. The third level institution are many. Priority (upto 50 yrs.) of India up to 2000 was to enhance social access and social equity in higher education.

Social Access

Social access means that I must have access to an institution of higher education close to where I live. I don't have to go from a small place to Allahabad or Varanasi. We have achieved social access and social equality in 50 yrs.

Indicators of Social Access

1. Number of universities & colleges
   * Number of universities (*e.g.* 296 upto 2003)
   * Number of colleges (12,000 upto 2003)
2. Number of students & teachers
   * Number of students (88, lakh upto 2003)
   * Number of teachers (4,75,000 upto 2003)
3. Rural Areas
   * Rural area has an institute of higher education within the radius of 100-120 KM

Number of Universities and Colleges in India.

YEAR	UNIVERSITIES	COLLEGES
1950	50 UNIVERSITIES	700 COLLEGES
2003	296	12,000 COLLEGES
YEAR	STUDENTS	TEACHERS
1950	ONE LAKH	15,000
2003	88 LAKHS	4, 75,000 UNIVERSITY & COLLEGE TEACHER

It ensures access to higher education but can not be considered less.

4. Semi-urban Areas
   * The range of distance of access to higher education is 60-80 KM in semi-urban areas
5. Urban Areas
   * The access to higher education in urban areas is 30-40 KM.
6. Increase in the First Higher Education Learners.

Percentage of first higher education learners is increasing. For example 22-23 percent of 88 lakh students (year 2003) are the first higher education learners. This percentage is increasing by half a percent every two years (1½% increase / 2 yrs.) Many people who are holding important positions in the country are first higher education learners in their families.

Need and Importance of Quality in Higher Education

There is improvement in social access and social equity after independence. Access ratio to higher education is only 7 per cent as compared to 30-60 per cent of developing countries. The efforts should continue towards social access and social equity but knowledge has become very important in our life today as a result of technological advancement or revolution in communication and information. The above factor "role of information today" has forced us to take care to quality factor in higher education also. This should be our top priority in higher education.

To quote Arun Nigavekar :

"Because acommunication and information revolution, knowledge has become very important. Therefore, quality of education has also become very important. This means that when we are in the first decade of the 21st century in addition to social access and social audit, access to information is important as also equity in reference to quality of education irrespective of one's geographical location. To meet this, we should provide information pathways at the door steps of higher education institutions. We will achieve this through UGC information network. We are also linking all the colleges with unlimited clockhour internet connectivity. "

Steps being taken by UGC, NIEPA and Central Government for Quality Improvement in Higher Education

UGC Support for Research Journal in Electronic Format. UGC is planning in the 10th plan to go in for subscription of research journals in electronic format. Negotiations are in progress with publishers. It is estimated that a university is spending about 70-80 lakhs per year on an average for journals. The cost-effective means are being searched. It is planned to adopt the system of bulk subscription will assure better access to information. Money can be saved. The saved money can be spent on purchase of textbooks and reference books.

Education Abroad. Indian higher education is good in terms of quality but the marketing is poor, steps should be taken in this direction.

NIEPA and Appointment of Teachers. Questions are there on the contract appointment or tenure track appointment (e.g. appointment for five years end and then renewal after academic appraisal as in Tamil Nadu, Andhra Pradesh, Maharashtra etc). National Institute of Education and Public Administration (NIEPA) is taking up the matter. Seminars, conferences and media views through various print media, electronic media etc. are being used for finding some well thought decision as an alternative to the present long-term appointment as permanent teachers. This is also a step towards improving quality of education at the higher level institutions in India.

Teaching Hours. Teaching hours in higher education institution is also an issue of hot discussion. Trend is to increase teaching hours e.g. 15 hours to 22 hours. Some universities like Delhi University is thinking about setting up a committee for taking decisions on academic reforms and accountability.

Specific Problems in Quality Control in Higher Education

Problem of Enrolment. Views of Education-Commission (1964-66) are mentioned below :

Selective Admission. Since the demand for enrolment to higher education will be much larger than the provision that can be made for it or is needed on the basis of man power needs, a system of selective admissions will have to be adopted.

Part-time Education. Opportunities for part time education (correspondence courses; evening colleges) should be extended widely and should include courses in science and technology.

College Size. A college should normally have a minimum of 500 and it would be preferable to raise it to 1000 or more.

Education of Women. At present the proportion of women students to men students in higher education is 1:4. This should be increased to about 1 : 3 to meet the requirements for educated women in different fields.

Study of Humanities. The need for strengthening the humanities cannot be overstressed. We should make significant contributions to the sum total of human knowledge and experience in the fields of the social and pedagogical science and humanistic studies, while our old traditions and the present challenges posed by social development present unique opportunities for creative work.

Educational Research. An Educational Research Council should be set up in the Ministy of Education for the promotion of research.

Problem of Examination

Reforms in examinations at the tertiary level are needed to improve the quality of education. Examinations have to be made reliable, continuous, comprehensive, creative, corrective and judicious. Reforms in examination system should be reflected in the syllabi, textbooks, methods of teaching and even school organisation.

The importance of examination for improving quality of education can be judged on the basis of views expressed by the following commissions :

1. Radhakrishnan Commission 1948. "If we are to suggest one single reform in university education, it should be that of examination."
2. Mudaliar Commission (1952-53). "The examinations determine not only contents of education, but also the methods of teaching, in fact entire approach to education."
3. The National Policy on Education 1986. "As part of sound educational strategy, examinations should be employed to bring about qualitative improvements in education."

National Policy on Education proposed the following points to reform examination system after due consideration of the defects in examination system :

1. The elimination of excessive element of chance and subjectivity.
2. The de-emphasis of memorisation.
3. Continuous and comprehensive evaluation that incorporates both scholastic and non-scholastic aspects of education spread over the total span of instructional time.

4. Effective use of the evaluation process by teachers, students and parents.
5. Improvement in the conduct of examination.
6. The introduction of concomitant changes in ins . urtional materials and methodology.
7. The introduction of semester system from the secondary stage in a phased manner and.
8. The use of gradation place of marks.

Problem of Establishment of Autonomous Colleges

Need of Autonomy

Increase in the Number of Institution: Concept of affliating universities was good for earlier conditions when the number of colleges and universities was less. Presently the number of higher institutions has increased. Institutions are acting as instruments of social change. Needs of Indian society are diverse. Problems are different. The institutions should be free to design educational courses meeting specific problems of the society. The affiliating system is infact an obstacle in the freedom of these institutions. The academic freedom (autonomy) must be given. The Education Commission (1964-66) regarded the exercise of academic freedom on the part of teachers as crucial to the promotion and development of an intellectual climate in the country which is conducive to the pursuit of scholarship and excellence.

To quote the Education Commission (1964-66):

"We should like to refer to the question of 'autonomous' colleges which has been under discussion for many years. Where there is an outstanding college or a small cluster of very good colleges within a large university which has shown the capacity to improve itself markedly, consideration should be given to granting it an autonomous status, this would involve the power to frame its own rules of admission, to prescribe its courses of study, to conduct examinations and so on. The parent university's role will be one of general supervision and the actual conferment of the degree. The privilege cannot be conferred once for all and it will have to be continually earned and deserved and it should be open to the university, after careful scrutiny of the position, to revoke the autonomous status if the college at any stage begins to deteriorate in its standards. We recommend that provisions for the recognition of such autonomous colleges be made in the constitution of the universities."

To quote National Policy on Education (1986):

"In view of mixed experiences with the system of affiliation, autonomous colleges will be helped to develop in large numbers until the affiliating system is replaced by a free and more creative association of universities with colleges. Similarly, the creation of autonomous departments within universities on a selective basis will be encouraged. Autonomy and freedom will be accompanied by accountability."

Aims and Objectives of Autonomy

The autonomous college is the current alternative to existing system of university in India. An autonomous college will have the freedom to :

(1) determine its own courses of study and syllabi;
(2) prescribe rules of admission, course, the reservation policy of the State Government; and
(3) evolve methods of evaluation and to conduct examinations.

Following are the aims of autonomous colleges.

Quality Control. The aim of the autonomy is to achieve higher standards and greater creativity in the future.

Aim of Promotion of National Integration The promotion of national integration will be an important aim of the autonomous colleges through academic programmes and other activities.

Redesigning of the Curriculum. UGC has recently redesigned higher education curriculum and circulated to all 296 Universities in India for compliance upto a specific period. Most of the universities have implemented these courses or have revised their educational programmes accordingly. Similarly, teaching-learning strategies are also being revised. New infrastructure is being developed. Thus quality control in the light of present and future needs are being maintained.

Decentralisation of Academic Administration. UGC is promoting the principle of decentralisation of academic administration. This policy of UGC will contribute to promote quality in higher education centre.

Promotion of Creativity, Innovation and Higher Standards. UGC & other higher education linked bodies are contributing significantly to promote creativity, innovation and higher standards. A brief description of a few such bodies with aims are described below:

University Grants Commission (UGC)

* UGC was established in 1956 under the Act of Parliament
* Main aims of UGC are :
    * taking of necessary steps to promote and coordinate university education
    * determination and maintenance of standards in teaching, examination and research.
    * assessment about financial requirements of universities.
    * establishment and maintenance of common services. Recently Arun Nigavekar has mentioned about UGC efforts to engage certain publishers to provide journals to universities in electronic form. These will save a lot of finances of the universities. It is estimated that each university spends about 70-80 lakhs each year for journals. There are 296 universities and 12000 colleges in India besides other special institutes. One can imagine the financial involvement only with specific reference to one item i.e. journal subscription per annum.
    * designing & recommending programmes for the improvement of university education.

  Recently, curriculum programmes have been circulated throughout the country for implementation. Current trends in curricular developments have been taken care of

* UGC has coordination with bodies like NAAC (National Assessment and Accreditation Council), NCTE, (National Council for Teacher Education), AICTE etc.

Indian Council of Historical Research (ICHR), New Delhi

* ICHR was established in 1972.
* Main aims of ICHR are to :

— review historical research;

— encourage scientific writing of history ;

— fund research projects by individuals;

— operate research projects;

— award fellowships;

— publish literature; and

— translate standard works.

Indian Council of Philosophical Research (ICPR)

— ICPR was set up in 1981 with offices in New Delhi and Lucknow.

— Main goals of ICPR are to :

— review the progress;

— sponsor or assist projects and programmes in philosophy; and

— finance/fund institutions and individuals for research activities in Philosophy & allied areas.

Indian Institute of Advanced Study (IIAS).

— It was set up in 1965 at Shimla. It is residential in nature.

— Main aims of IIAS are to :

— promote a community of scholars who are interested in exploration, questions of inter-disciplinary nature and questions of contemporary relevance.

Indian Council of Social Science Research (ICSSR)

— It is an autonomous body with Headquarter at New Delhi.

— Main goals of this body are to :

— promote and science research;

— review progress of social science research ;

— give advice on research activities to Government of India and other interested bodies in India;

— Sponsor research programmes; and

— give grants to institutions and individuals for research activities.

NAAC (National Accreditation and Assessment Council). The National Accreditation and Assessment Council makes an assessment of the higher education institution and issues accreditation certificate on the basis of well defined criteria. Thus, the council helps in quality control of centres of higher learning.

QUESTIONS

1. Discuss the views of various Commissions/National Policy on Education 1986 on the quality control in higher education institutions
2. Discuss your views on the quality control in higher education in India
3. Discuss the views of Arun Nigavekar the present UGC Chairman on the quality of higher education in India
4. Describe problems of quality control in higher education in India.
5. Comment upon the following
   (1) Autonomous colleges and quality control in higher education
   (2) Examination reforms and quality control in higher education
   (3) Problem of enrolment in higher education & quality control
   (4) Quality control in higher education & promotion of creativity and research.

17

Integration through Education

In Indian society, the development of emotional and national integration is one of the aim of education. Indian culture is a composite one problems are there because of the factors like difference in languages of different states regionalism, casteism, variety of value systems, religious differences etc. The instances are there before independence and after independences, when these factors attacked the unity of the nation. Feelings of disintegration developed because of the anti-national forces. These factors are the major ones to be handled. It is a hard fact, that every nation has specific common aspects crossing all sorts of diversities. There is always a unity in divresity or there is always a diversity in a unity. This is the universal law. We have to understand this law. The lack of ignorance of this fact lead us to an undesirable situation i.e. the troubled India. There are a number of steps to handle this problem. The feelings of the composite culture or pluristic Indian society can be integrated through education as an instrument. Present chapter deals with the problem of en Monal and national integration and the role of education to solve the same.

Meaning of Emotional Integration and National Integration

Bhatnagar (1983). To quote Bhatnagar (1983) p 701:

"Emotional integration is the sentiment which consigns oblivion the linguistic, racial, religious and other differences between various communities and welds them into a single unity. Thus it implies an attitude or mental state which rises above all differences of caste and class, and which binds in a single bond, the people of different religions, communities and languages. The term emotional intergration is based upon both for the individual as well as the human group.

For the individual emotional integration can be taken to mean a completely balanced personality, whose desires, ambitions, and emotions all direct themselves to useful and positive ends, a personality in which there is tolerance and restraint. In the same way an emotionally integrated group is aware of its country as a single entity. It leavs behind all affliations of community, languages or region. It generates a common faith for the country and its populace."

To quote S. Bhatnagar (1983 P 702):

"Emotional integration provides the foundation for national integration when the citizens of a country come to experience emotional inegration, they also develop a tendency to sacrifice their private and narrow interests in order to bring about national progress. In short, national integration can be viwed as a feeling which encourages people to have the same affection for every piece in the country and also to care for the interests of the entire nation. The aim of national integration is to bring the people of a country into a single entity."

Aims of national integration are:

1. To maintain unity.
2. To contribute to the social and economic development of the country.
3. To make national life prosperous and rich by developing culture of various communities.
4. To check the fissiparious tendencies among the various communities of the country.

Brubacher. "Nationalism ordinarily indicates a wider scope of loyality than patriotism in addition to ties of place. Nationality is evidenced by such ties as race, language, history, culture, and tradition."

Humayun Kabir. "Nationalism is that which depends on we-feeling towards the nation.

Dorothy Thompson. "National integration is a feeling that blinds the citizens of a country."

Hitler. "My country good or bad, should be dear to me."

Kothari Commission (1964-66). "National integration includes a confidence in nation's future, a continuous rise in the standard of living, development of feeling of values and duties, a good and impartial administrative system and mutual understanding."

Narrow and Broader Meaning of Nationalism

Nationalism (national integration) should not be taken in the narrow sense i.e. taking a rigid stand to blind to one nation. No nation can not remain isolated today. In the global village, all nations are interrelated and interdependant and hence the changes in one nation affect the development in other nations of the world. The rigidities for a nation without bothering about the reality of inter-relationship and interdependence are harmful for all. So national integration (nationalism) as a feeling in a accordance with international understanding or international peace (internationalism) in good or we can say thinking national integration in this our look may be called as taking meaning of national integration in a broader sense. Similarly, taking the meaning negatively the meaning of the term is taken in the narrow sense. To quote Mudalliar Commission (1952-53).

"There is no more dangerous maxim in the world of today then. My country right or wrong. The white world in now so intimately interconnected that no nation can or dare live alone and the development of a sense of world citizenship has become just as important as that of national citizenship."

To Quote Jawahar Lal Nehru:

"Nationalism is such a strange element which while it instils life, development and integration, at the same time makes it narrow because on account of it a person thinks about his own country as separate from other countries of the world."

Need of Emotional and National Integration

Need to Check Negative Forces/Tendencies. Follows factor's concerning modem society serve as indicators of feeling of disinteration which is serious for the existence or survival of man kind:

1. Frustration/psychological barriers.
2. Lack of political leadership in the country.

3. Public clashes/violence.
4. Lack of patriotism or taking patriotism in the narrow sense.
5. Casteism as a factor for development hatred.
6. Regionalism as a Factor in the development of negative feelings.
7. Language as the factor of developing negative feeling.
8. Geographical factors as barriers of integration.
9. Regional cultural & social variations as barriers.
10. Rigidities of values as barriers.
11. Ignorance of the significance of international understanding.
12. Ignorance about factors that affect national development today.

Recommendations of Kothari Commission (1964-66). National understanding or national integration is essential and one of aim of education. National integration implies:

1. A confidence in the nations, future.
2. A continuous rise in the standard of living for the masses which included reduction in unemployment.
3. A deep sense of values and obligations of citizenship and growing identification of the people not with national loyalities but with nation as a whole.
4. Mutual understanding and respect for the culture, tradition and ways of life among different sections of the people. Only a united nation can stand firmly like pillars to shoulder any type of outer or inner threats of its existence. The present situations that prevail all around further necessitate to have a strong united nations.

Dr. Radhakrishnan. "If India is to remain free, united and democratic , education should train people for unity and not localism, for democracy and not dictatorship."

Pandit Jawaharlal Nehru. "We should not become parochial, narrow-minded provinced communal and caste-minded, because we have a great mission to perform. Let us, the citizens of the

Republic of India, bring about the integration of Indian people. We have to build up this great country into a mighty nation, mighty not in the oridinary sense of the word, but mighty in action, mighty in culture and mighty in its peaceful service of humanity."

Emotional Integration Leads to National Integration

Emotional integration is the prerequisite of national integration or we can say that emotional integration is the foundation on which national integration stands.

To Quote Pandit Nehru:

"Let us, the citizens of the Republic of India stand up with straight backs and look up at the skies, keeping our feet firmly planted on the ground and bring about the synthesis, the integration of the Indian people. Political integration has already taken place, but what I am after is something deeper than that, an emotional integration of the Indian people so that we may be welded into one strong national unit, maintaining at the same time all our wonderful diversity."

Disruptive and Separatist Elements/Factors of Emotional and National Integration in India

Certain factors/forces/ elements/problems act as disruptive and separatist factors/elements/forces and thus challenge the emotional and national integration in India. Four major problems are briefly described here:

The Sentiment of Communalism. There are a number of communities in our country due to variety of value system i.e Hinduism, Islam, Christianity, Jainism, Buddhism, Sikhism etc. Certain individuals groups/forces try to develop situation which are conflicting & generate an environment of hatred among citizens belonging to different value systems. The sentiments/emotions are exploited for one factor or the other. As a result of this many observations are recorded e.g killings, damage of property, strikes, closure of shops, industries etc. We have to take appropriate steps for checking such forces.

Problem of Language Differences. There are a number of modem Indian languages and dialects. Sometimes, situations are created, when we feel low or high only on the basis of use of language e.g. state language, official language, medium of instruction. All languages are equally important. The equality factor is knowingly ignored. Emotions of the people are exploited on certain vested interests. This situation should be avoided otherwise national development will be slow.

Problem of Regionalism/Provincialism. Rigidities or bases for specific regions are ultimately harmful for all of us. Every state or the region is important for its specific characteristics. Today, we can survive only if we follow the concept of a system. In a system, there is a set of component parts which are interelated and interdependent & the overall objective of the system depends upon the required role of every component. Similarly, the country is like a system, every component state is to play the required role and thus national development is possible. Regionalism i.e behaviour like "my state is the best" is harmful and it is a big problem.

Remedial Measures for Development of Emotional and National Integration in India

Recommendations of Dr. Sampurnanand Committee. According to the report of the Sampurananand Committe, following steps through Indian system of education may prove to be helpful in developing emotional and nation integration :

Adequate Changes in the Syllabus & Text Books. Revision in the syllabus & text books can help in achieving the desired results.

Organisation of Meetings. One or two meeting of parents students and teachers should be organised that may highlight the significance of emotional and national integration.

National Anthem and Prayer. National anthem & prayer should be the integral part of morning assembly.

Organisation of Extra-curricular Activities. Organisation of following activities contribute to the development of emotional and national integration :

* National festivals
* Birthday celebrations of national leaders & great men of the nation.

* NCC activities
* Scouting activities
* Educational tours
* Games
* Cultural programmes like youth festivals
* Religious festival

Teaching of National History, Geography and Culture. The teaching of varied aspects of the nation develop love for the nation. Religious democratic & secular values should be emphasized.

Recommendations of Emotional Integration Committee (1961)

Development of General Policy of Education. A national educational policy should be developed & some uniform framework will contribute to think in one direction by all States.

Three Language Formula. Three language formuala should be implemented

(a) Mother tongue/regional language

(b) Official language or supplementary official language

One Modem Indian Language or Foreign Language (Excluding English). At the lower Primary level, mother tongue should be taught. Mother tongue or regional language and Hindi or English should be taught at the upper primary level. Three language should be taught at the lower secondary level, (mother language or regional language ; Hindi and English.

A Special Subject at Higher Education Level. Some course should be designed & offered at the higher level that may help in developing feelings for the nation.

Improvement of Teacher's Salary. Improvement in the pay scale of teachers may increase their involvement & dedication towards work.

Opportunities for Students. Diversification of courses (professional & training should be there for students

Scholarships. Scholarships for students should be adequate.

Admission. Admission should not be on the basis of caste & place of birth

Hindi. Teaching of Hindi must be encouraged.

English. English should be taught as a link language.

History. Proper arrangement should be there for teaching of Indian History.

Contribution of the Teachers & Heads

Teaching staff & heads of the institutions are at the grassroot level and implement the policies of the Government & recommendation of various committees/commissions. The curricular & co-curricular activities should be centred around the development of feelings of oneness.

Evolving a National System of Education

Steps by Central Govt. have been taken under the New Policy on Education-1986 for streamlining the national system of education. Currently (2000), each State has taken decision on the State Education Policy. Every educational policy (statewise) is taking care of this aspect in view.

Economic Development Policies/National Development Policies

Policies of the Government take special consideration of the factor of national integration because collective efforts only can bring results and improve our standards of living.

Improvement in the Provisions for Teachers, Students & other Educational Professionals

A variety of provisions for teachers, principals, and students can help in the generation of an environment that may develop love for the nation. Investment by the nation to improve the standard of living of all citizens definitely shows positive & equal response by citizens towards the nation.

QUESTIONS

1. Discuss the meaning of national integration and emotional integration.
2. Discuss the need of emotional and national integration with specific reference to India.
3. Comment upon the following :

   "Emotional integration leads to national integration."
4. Comment upon factors responsible for attacking the national and emotional integrity of the Indian nation.
5. Discuss the remedial measures for the achievement of aim of national and emotional integration.